THE BEAST IN THE CREASE:

A LACROSSE GOALIE'S GUIDEBOOK

by
Fritz Hoffecker

THE BEAST IN THE CREASE

ISBN 978-0-6152-2197-7

Contents

Acknowledgements

I couldn't have written this book without the following people:

- My teammates over the past 45 years, who have stuck together even through a difficult season or two, had a good time, worked hard and showed me how well the game can be played.
- My coaches who, over the years, have encouraged me, challenged me, and helped me work through the bad days.
- My late father, who played at St. John's in the early '30s.
- My uncle, Tom Hoffecker, a 3-time All American goalie at Maryland, and my second cousin, Tommy Gough, an All American at Hopkins, who were modest about their own talents, but inspired me to keep working hard at becoming a better goalie.
- My son, Tom Hoffecker, an excellent goalie himself, who helped me with the text and photos – and taught me a lot of new things about playing goalie, even at my advanced age.
- My daughter, Margaret Hoffecker, who had the patience to take some of the photos.

A Note about the Photos

Tom, Margaret and I took all the photos in this book, except for the old ones, which various people - I've forgotten who - gave me over the years. The quality and clarity of some of the game pictures that I took aren't that great, but are good enough to get across some points that I'm trying to make. I "brushed out" the numbers of all the players (except Tom) because in some cases I've pointed out mistakes that a player is making, e.g., standing flat-footed, and I don't want to pick on specific individuals.

Why a book?

In this age of videos and DVD's, you might wonder why I've written a 200-page book about playing goalie instead of trying to put a few lessons on tape. My feeling is that the reader can go over a section of this book at his own speed, spend more or less time on specific areas, and study the diagrams and photos as much as he likes. He can then go out and practice what he's just learned, and easily come back and reference any area that's giving him trouble. As he moves from section to section, he'll find more and more areas he can add to his practice sessions. The sections try to build from basic fundamentals (watching the ball, stance, stepping, etc.) to more complex areas like clears and man-down. Finally, I get into practice and pre-game prep routines that have worked for me and many others. A book may be "old technology," but I think it can help in ways that are different from videos. DVD's and VCR's are great too, and obviously offer the advantage of showing goalies in action. I recommend using them and every other tool you can get your hands on. Then go out and practice, work hard, have fun.

1

Getting Started

This book is geared toward anybody – player, coach, young, old – who is thinking about playing or coaching goalie in lacrosse or has already done so for a year or three. That makes the book geared mostly to youth league and high schoolers – and their coaches. I'll cover a lot of critical basic techniques, and the best time to learn and practice them is when you're young. But even those with several years of experience might find this a good place to re-check their fundamentals, and pick up a few new ideas.

There's a lot of material in this book. If you're just starting out in the goal, I recommend that you take it in small doses, work on a section at a time, move on to the next section, and occasionally go back to earlier parts to see if you've forgotten anything. For example, read about watching the ball and do some of the activities I've suggested for improving in this area. Then read about the stance, practice dropping into a perfect stance for a day or so. Move on to Stepping, and work on that for a couple days – but on Day 2, go back to your stance to make sure you haven't forgotten something.

If you've played goalie for a couple years already, you can still keep getting better at the basics and also work on some of the more advanced techniques.

Coaches and parents might also learn a thing or two. Nothing can ruin a goalie faster than bad coaching or a well-intentioned but misguided, misinformed parent. I was exposed to a lot of bad goalie coaching when I was younger, so I'd like to educate coaches so they're better equipped to help their goalies by putting in useful drills and teaching solid fundamental techniques. Groups like the Positive Coaching Alliance (PCA) have broader advice for coaches and parents, and I recommend that you check them out. Their approach applies to all sports and all positions, while I'll focus specifically on what's good and not good for helping goalies get better – including what coaches should and shouldn't do for and to their keepers.

All goalies and all coaches won't agree with everything I recommend. Wherever possible, I've noted areas that are controversial and where things can be done in more than one way. But I'm sure I've missed a few, and some experts (both real and imagined) will disagree with me here and there. That's one thing that makes playing goalie so interesting and challenging: There's no single best way to do everything. Each goalie will develop his own style, based on his own particular set of skills and experiences. In this book I offer a lot of solid fundamentals, plus what's worked well for me - and I suggest that you work hard and try different things to see what works best for you.

Girls' and Women's Lacrosse

I don't know much about the women's game, so I've geared this book to men's lacrosse. For that reason, I've used masculine pronouns and words throughout ("he," "him,"

2

"man"). However, I've watched some girls and women play ball, and I suspect that playing goalie and making saves is similar to the men's game. I hope that some young female goalies will learn something from the book, and not be put off by all the "he's" and "him's."

My experience

So why should you listen to me? You might have had other instructors before, and I'm sure many of them were top-notch. But if you're anything like me, you'll always listen to other goalies and try out additional techniques to see if they work for you.

I'm not the greatest goalie that ever played the game, by any means. I could give you a long list of guys who are more famous and successful than I've been. But to try to look frankly at my game, I think I can honestly say that I've been pretty good at a lot of different skill levels – high school, Division I, and club. I have some weaknesses, which I still work on, but I never reveal these in public, in case there's an opponent out there trying to figure out how to beat me with his next shot. Yes, I've had some average games, but I've also had some great ones. Yes, I've blown the easy save a time or two, but I've also made some tough ones. Overall, I've always had a fairly good all-around game. At age 58, my body can't always do what I tell it to as fast as I used to, but solid fundamentals, decent conditioning, and intense focus have kept me competitive.

My experience?

High School: As a 12-year-old in 1962, I started out as a center middie at Chestertown (Md.) High School, which included grades 7 through 12. In those days, even a 7th grader could play varsity if he was good enough. I ran first midfield and faced off, but stepped in the goal for the last couple games of the season. After one of those games, I was offered a scholarship to Boys' Latin, one of Baltimore's traditional powerhouses, but I'd already committed to a different boarding school, which didn't have lacrosse.

College: I played other sports in high school, but always planned to try lacrosse again in college, so in my freshman year at Princeton, I walked on and beat out six other goalies to become starter on a really strong freshman team (those were the days when freshman weren't allowed to play varsity).

I was third team varsity the next year and started on an undefeated JV team. After a Junior Year of studying overseas, I started for most of my senior year, before getting injured. Unfortunately, a lot of guys had quit the team during the tumultuous early 70's, and we stunk, going 1-11. At least we were losing to the best teams in the country: Virginia, Navy and Army all whipped us, but we played Hopkins close. I can still see those Maryland guys running in undefended and firing at me! If you play goalie, you're going to have days – and seasons - like that.

<u>Club:</u> After college, I played club ball from 1971 to today (2007), with a few years off for working overseas. I've played on some great squads, and some with little talent. My teams have gone undefeated and even winless (once). Some of my teammates and opponents have been fairly new to the game, but many have been D1 and D3 studs, plus a lot of All-Americans. At this point, I've just finished a couple good seasons – my Grand Masters team (over 45) beat our strongest rival, and in a different league, my Open (over 18 – mostly guys in their 20's) squad went undefeated. For the most part, I played pretty well and had a good time. In February one of the pro teams, the Washington Bayhawks, invited me to a tryout. We scrimmaged for a couple hours, and I held up pretty well against some of the nation's top young players. Yes, I let in a couple goals but also had some nice saves. I didn't make the Bayhawks, but why would they want a 58-year-old goalie? In any case, I had a good time, and it was great to be on the field with so many top-notch players.

I don't want to be one of those athletes who tries to hang on too long, so am thinking about hanging up the spikes. Tearing my ACL in May 2005 was a challenge, but I came back after many months of rehab. But before I leave the game, and while some games are still fresh in my mind, I've decided to pass along a few of the things I've learned. At one time or another, I've played all the positions – as an attackman, I even scored 4 goals in a quarter once (ok, so the other team wasn't very good) – but Goalie has always been the most exciting and fun. It's hard and demands tremendous training, dedication, athleticism and leadership, but I have no regrets. For those of you just starting, or in your first couple years, I hope you learn something from this book, and I wish you the best of luck. Read on…and then get out there and practice.

Why be a Goalie?

I've played many sports in my life – baseball, football, soccer, wrestling - and there's nothing quite like being a goalie in lacrosse. It can be physically and mentally tough, but there's a lot of action and includes all the things I like to do – make saves, run, pass, and contribute to a team.

In my opinion, it's also not only the most challenging position in lacrosse, but certainly one of the most challenging in any sport. You have to have:

- Exceptional reflexes,
- Good footspeed,
- Great stickwork,
- Advanced leadership skills,
- An understanding of everything that's going on on the field,
- Day-to-day, week-to-week, month-to-month and even year-to-year discipline,
- A strong work ethic,
- A positive attitude and
- No fear…

…all in one person. All of us goalies fall short in some of these categories, but that just means there's always something to work harder on.

Don't even bother to strap on the chest protector if you don't like the idea of practicing and spending a lot of time on your game to keep getting better. It's not a position for the spoiled egocentric kid, who won't put in the extra effort, and just wants all the glory of making a great save every now and then.

I've seen a lot of kids who had some early success in the cage and stopped working. They initially got by on natural reflexes. But when they tried to go to the next level – from Under 13 to Under 15, from youth league to high school, from high school to college – they found that good reflexes alone aren't enough. They hadn't worked hard enough on their fundamentals, and were immediately overmatched. Believe me, if you have a weakness, your opponent will find it fast and make the most of it – especially as you move to higher skill levels or if other teams scout you. End of career, unless you decide to get back to work.

Note that when I say "work," I don't mean it as a negative. After all, lacrosse is a sport to be enjoyed. Personally, I enjoy it more if I play well than if I play poorly. And the best way to play well is to practice and spend time on your game. This book will talk about a lot of areas that you can think about, practice and work on. I don't pretend to know everything, but in 45 years I've learned a few things that I think are useful and generally hold true.

Why you need to "do it right" and practice

If you haven't played much in the goal, you might say to yourself: "Hey I'm a pretty good athlete, with really good reflexes. Why can't I just hop in the goal and immediately be good?"

First, we're dealing in shots going 80 or 90 miles per hour, and the difference between a save and a goal can be just that $1/100^{th}$ of a second.

Here's something to think about:
- A 90-mph shot goes 132 feet per second
- From 30 feet, 90-mph shot takes 0.227 second to reach the goal.
- From 20 feet, it takes 0.15 second.
- An 80-mph shot goes 117 feet per second
- From 30 feet, 80-mph shot takes 0.256 second to reach the goal.
- From 20 feet, it takes 0.17 second.

Figure 1 below shows these shot speeds and time-to-goal.

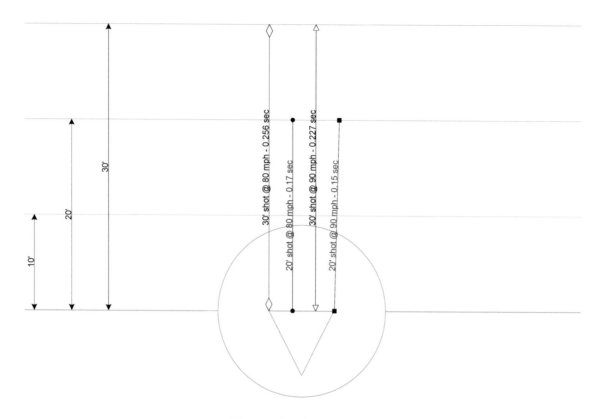

Figure 1 – Shot Speeds

First - Improving the time it takes to make a save

If you don't have a good idea of how fast a tenth or two tenths of a second are, then try this experiment. Get a stopwatch that will start when you push a button, and then stop when you push it a second time. Do it as fast as you can, and see how much time elapses between the first and second pushes. I've tried this on a digital stopwatch and never gotten below 0.07 second. You have only two or three times that long to see the shot and make a complete save move.

One of my primary objectives in this book is to shave 100ths of a second off the time it takes for a goalie to react to the shot, make the right "save move," and make the save.

Every item I talk about is important in keeping this time to a minimum and making you faster. For example, take the section on "Stance": Being back on your heels can cost you, say, 0.05 second. Having your stickhead in the wrong place can cost another 0.03 second. Take the "Watch the Ball" section: Not watching the ball properly can add another 0.05. If you start to add all these mistakes up, the ball gets by you.

6

Second - Beyond the Save: Running the D, Passing, Clearing, etc. etc.

Second, there's a lot more to being a goalie than just making saves. You need to run the defense, run the clears, make good passes, avoid stupid mistakes, keep your teammates on task, and so on. You need to figure out what the opponent is trying to do and counteract it – this often means going to your coach with a suggestion (like, we ought to put Joe on Number 6, or switch to a zone, or whatever).

What's in the book

Following is a list of subjects covered in this book.

1.   Attitude - team first, sportsmanship
2.   Equipment
3.   Focus – always be ready, pay attention
4.   Watch the BALL
5.   Stance
6.   Position & moving on the arc
7.   Stepping to the ball
8.   Goalie stickwork: Making the save, passing & catching
9.   Talk - running the defense:
10. Clearing
11. Conditioning for goalies (subject to coaches' and parents' ok)
12. Man-down
13. Fast breaks
14. One-on-ones
15. Dealing with screens
16. Temptation
17. Get to know your opponent
18. Practice for Goalies
19. Pre-game prep
20. Personal Techniques

It might look like a lot, but – as I mentioned earlier - I suggest approaching the material a step at a time: Read a section, think about it, maybe write a note or two in the margin, and then practice what's suggested. Try to get better at each area (e.g., Stance, Stepping to the ball, etc.) before moving on to the next. You can practice things like stepping to the ball and passing every day of your life and still have room for improvement.

Eventually you'll find drills and ways to practice that incorporate most or at least many of the subjects in a single day or two. But you can work up to that slowly. Get started in the off-season. In the winter, if you devote even a half hour a day to conditioning and a half hour to technique, you'll be surprised at how much better you can get by the time the season starts in the spring.

Muscle memory

One important note about practicing and drills: Especially early in your career, one of your main goals is to build the correct "muscle memory" for each key move. For example, when you move to make an offside low save, you want all your muscles – the ones that control your feet, legs, hands, arms, neck, etc. – to be doing the right thing, in the right sequence, at the right time. Having the best muscle memory just means that you've practiced the correct save move so much that your muscles have "memorized" everything correctly, and you can do the whole thing automatically and really fast.

A basketball foul shot is an example: The best foul shooters do the same thing, move their same muscles the same way (or very close to it) every time. Their muscles have "memorized" what to do.

Likewise, as a goalie, you want to train your muscles to automatically do the right things to make the save. On a shot, seeing the ball leave the stick is the "cue" that should set your muscles into the right moves that they've "memorized." That's one reason you'll see me emphasize watching the ball so much. The faster you can pick up the shot leaving the stick, the faster your muscles can be "cued" to go into the right "memorized" moves.

For me, the best way to build and improve muscle memory is the following:

1) First you have to learn what the correct moves are for each type of shot. I'll talk about this later in the book. There's no point in becoming fast at a bad move, so learn to do it right the first time.

2) Second, with all your gear on but without getting shot at, start to make this move slowly, one step at a time. Go slowly until you think you're doing the move correctly. You probably need somebody – preferably an experienced goalie - to watch and help you make adjustments.

3) Third, without being shot at, repeat the move many times, gradually going faster and faster.

4) Next, get in the cage, and have somebody shoot at you so that you can practice that same move. They can start shooting fairly slowly and gradually increase the speed. Get feedback from an experienced goalie if at all possible.

5) Finally, you get to do all your save moves in practice, scrimmages and games.

I use a similar approach for learning to pass, catch, scoop, dodge and so on:

1) Learn how to do it right.

2) Do it slowly, a step at a time, by yourself, but with a more experienced person watching to give you feedback on your form.

3) Do it faster and faster, and/or harder and harder, until you reach game-level intensity.

4) Do it in game-simulation conditions (drills, practice).

5) Do it in scrimmages, practice and games.

As you read through this book, try this same approach when you come to something new. If you start to build the proper muscle memory early in your career, it'll provide a great foundation for continuing to improve.

1.0 Attitude

Before I get into technique…my experience is that the head is just as important to a goalie as the rest of the body. What's going on inside the brain will have a powerful effect on how successful you become, not only at playing goalie but at being a good teammate.

Lacrosse is a team sport. No single player is going to win or lose a game alone. Yes, a goalie with 25 saves has made a great contribution to a win. But that goalie didn't take every face-off, score all the goals, and get every ground ball. On the other hand, the goalie who lets in a losing goal in the last 5 seconds didn't cause the loss single-handedly. Other players made bad passes, missed shots, scooped poorly, and maybe didn't guard that shooter very well at the end.

What does this mean for a goalie? I'll make a few general comments and then look at some specific situations.

1.1 Team and sportsmanship first

<u>Show good sportsmanship to your teammates, coach, opponents, fans and refs</u>: Yes, they can all be annoying sometimes, but you can rise above that – the simplest way I've found is to just keep my mouth shut when they go off the rails. I leave the trash-talking, end-zone dances and hot-dogging to somebody else.

1.1.1 Teammates

<u>Support your teammates:</u> Don't criticize them, blame them for your own mistakes, and yell at them (even when they screw up).

- If you play goalie, the following will happen to you, probably at least once a game: One of your defensemen messes up – slips, isn't paying attention, forgets to slide, whatever – and gets beat. The attackman comes around the corner and scores easily. You never had a chance. And, yes, it was all the D-man's fault. So what do you do?

- To answer this, put yourself in his place: How would you like to be treated?

- Here's what I do: If I think the guy knows what he did wrong, I just say something like, "Hey no sweat, Joe, you'll get him next time."

  If I feel he needs to think about what he messed up, I'll say, "OK, what happened?" Then he has to think about it, analyze at least a little bit, and come up with an answer. Usually, he'll know exactly what went wrong and will say,

"Yeah, I was slow to move with him" or "I overcommitted too soon." Then I'll say, "OK, you'll get him next time."

If he has no clue what he did wrong, then I'll have to tell him what he did wrong and what he should have done – not in a mean sarcastic way – I just try to be firm, plain and direct. If he never gets better, keeps making the same mistakes over and over, and/or has a bad attitude, then I suggest talking with your coach – in private – and asking him to give somebody else a chance.

<u>Attitudes are contagious</u>: If you're whining, negative and complaining a lot, this will rub off on some of your teammates. If you're positive, upbeat and show some sense of humor, this will also rub off. Who would you rather play with?

By being positive, I don't mean that you have to be a real "rah rah" type who goads everybody all day long. We had a guy like that in college, and after three weeks, everybody hated his guts. His self-righteousness caused more negative feelings than if he'd just kept his mouth shut. There's a fine line between being upbeat and being <u>too</u> upbeat. I try to keep it positive without overdoing it to the point of being a pain.

<u>Hard work in practice will pay off in games</u>: If you slack off in a drill, you're hurting yourself and your team. If you push yourself, you'll get better and probably lead your teammates to push themselves too.

<u>Work through the plateaus:</u> Sometimes you'll find that you're making good progress through the first 3 or 4 weeks of the season and then seem to either regress or not improve. You've reached a "plateau." The usual reaction is to panic, desert your fundamentals, and start trying off-the-wall techniques, such as "OK, every time a guy winds up from the outside, I'm going to guess that he'll shoot high."

This flailing around for a miracle cure never works. All goalies hit plateaus and even bad weeks when nothing seems to go right. My experience is that the best approach when I hit a plateau or a rough week is as follows:

1) Get somebody to watch me warm up and practice to check and see if I'm doing anything fundamentally wrong (e.g., not stepping, moving my head, getting in a bad stance). It's easy to accidentally drop into a bad habit or two, and I have to continually check to make sure my fundamentals are solid. If I find something that's "off," I work especially hard at getting back in the right groove.

2) Getting some film of practice or games and even some still photos can also help with this analysis.

3) Even if I can't find anything obviously wrong, I go back to the basics, which I'll discuss throughout this book: Stance, watching the ball, maintaining focus, position on the arc, stepping to the ball, etc.

11

4) Watch some top-level goalies play. This might show me what I'm doing wrong or trigger some ideas about how I can improve.

5) Take a full day off from lacrosse. Athletes can get stale, including goalies. There's no substitute for intelligent hard work, but every now and then it helps to forget the pressure of making saves, go to a movie, go bowling, read a book, whatever. I've found that some of my most productive insights have come out of the blue, while not even thinking about lacrosse.

<u>Keep working hard through the down years</u>: Your team won't win a championship every year. In fact, you might not even have a .500 record every year. But even when your record is 2-5, and the practices seem to be getting longer and longer, it's best to keep a positive attitude and be a good teammate. One of my son's teams had a so-so 8-8 record one season, worked through it, hung together, and won the State Championship the next year.

1.1.2 Coaches

Like you, the coach wants to have a good time, win games and see you get better. But there might be times when you don't like him much. He's making you run too much, has a lousy game plan, and spends all day screaming at everybody. Hint: Yelling back at him won't help.

Getting into a big argument in front of the whole team is seldom productive. Instead, if you have problems with or suggestions for the coach, you can ask to meet with him before or after practice to talk openly about whatever is bothering you. You can do this in private or take along the team captain(s) or other teammates if you think that would help to make a point.

If you have specific criticisms, then offer him suggestions about what you think would work better and why. In other words, don't just complain: Offer better ideas.

However, if a coach is truly abusive, such as hitting players, then you need to go to a parent or school authorities and report it.

1.1.3 Refs

This one is simple: Never argue with a call. In 45 years, I've seen a ref change a call about twice. Even when he knows he blew it, he still won't change it. If you argue and make a big stink, he'll remember you and not give you a break next time. I've seen that happen 100's of times. The odds are clearly in favor of biting your tongue.

In the course of 99% of games, the good and bad calls even out between the two teams. What's more, getting riled up about a call uses up a lot of energy and usually will rob you of your focus, which is something we goalies need in spades. It also distracts your teammates; half of them will agree with you that it was a bad call and will lose focus, and the other half will think you're acting like a jerk, and they'll also lose focus.

Win or lose, good calls or bad, I thank the refs after the game, first because it's good sportsmanship and second because he might be reffing my next game! I'd rather have a ref remember me for my sportsmanship, not my insults.

1.1.4 Fans

Hundreds of fans will be sorry to learn that every time they screamed "You stink goalie!" at me, instead of feeling bad about how lousy I was, I never even heard them. In fact, I never heard much of anything that fans were yelling, hopefully because I was focusing on playing ball.

But as a goalie, you have to be ready for that day when you get scored on and hear a fan yell out some clever comment like, "You stink goalie. My baby daughter could've saved that one." (This often comes from one of your own team's fans or one of your teammate's parents.) How do you react? It's natural to want to defend yourself or at least yell back, "OK fatso, you're so great, why don't *you* come out here and get in the goal."

My advice is to just suck it up and ignore it. You're doing your best, the fan is a jerk, and you're not. The main thing is to not let it get under your skin and ruin your concentration. If you're so mad that you just have to say something, pull one of your D-men aside and tell him what you think of the fat-mouth dork in the stands. You'll feel better – then drop it and get on with the game.

1.1.5 Parents

If you haven't graduated from high school or college yet, you might be getting a lot of lacrosse advice – maybe too much – from your parents. I don't want to get in the middle of how parents raise their kids, but here's my take.

To the kids: Your parents have good intentions – they want you to do well and have a good time. If your parents are on your case all the time or have unrealistic expectations of you and your team, take some time to explain to them what you and the squad are working on, why the drills and practices should make you better, and why you're not going to beat Giant High School this year because they have 6 All-Americans and you don't have any.

Most parents don't know all that much about lacrosse, so feel free to educate them. Go to some college games with them, where they'll see some really great players, and realize that the best players in the sport have all the athleticism, speed, strength and size of many professional athletes. Do they expect you to become starter at Syracuse? Well, that's almost the same as expecting you to become a starter for the USC football team. Watching top-level lacrosse will help them to put your abilities into the overall context of the game. They might also learn to appreciate you and your team more when you play well.

This is my advice to parents: Support your kids in lacrosse – it's a great sport where they can learn a lot about teamwork, selflessness, discipline, conditioning, and good sportsmanship. I think it's realistic for parents to expect their kids to go to practice, try hard, work hard, support their teammates, and be good sports. If your son isn't doing all that, then you might want to have a word with him.

If your kid has some talent and puts in a lot of time and energy, then he has a chance to play varsity in high school, and maybe in college. But let's face it – most kids don't become starters at Hopkins or Virginia, so don't put too much pressure on him. Lacrosse is fun to play, so let him enjoy it without a lot of badgering from you.

If he doesn't make the JV or varsity high school team, or even the college squad, I suggest not treating it as a failure. The world is full of kids who fell short one year, gave up, and never tried again. I don't think this is the life lesson you'd want to impart, i.e., "If you fail, give up." The world is also full of kids who didn't make the team one year but kept working hard throughout the year – conditioning, passing, catching, scooping, etc. - and came back to make the squad the following spring. One good thing about lacrosse is that many youth leagues have a "no cuts" policy, so if your son doesn't make the high school team, he can still hone his skills in a youth league. Many areas also have year-round club leagues (including indoor ball in the winter). In my experience, these teams never cut anybody. Club ball is a great opportunity to improve his skills, meet new people, and have a good time. I've seen new, raw players join a club team and get a lot better by the end of the season. Just being on the field with good players – plus ongoing practice – can have a really positive effect. So if your pride and joy gets cut from Varsity, give him a pat on the back for trying hard, encourage him to not quit, and help him find another place to play.

When you're watching a game, don't yell anything negative at your son, his teammates, the refs, the coaches or the opponents. There's nothing more embarrassing for a player than having his big-mouthed mom yelling at a ref about a game she's never even played. And you'll just be making a fool of yourself.

1.2 Attitude - Drills

So other than trying the things listed above to keep up a good attitude, what else can you do? Here are a few ideas:

Figure 1-1: No Whining

- Go an entire day without saying anything negative about anybody or anything. At the end of the day, review what happened and see how you did. This might sound a little corny, but you could be surprised to see what changes when you stop complaining. You don't have to be Little Mary Sunshine – just leave the bad attitude for a while.

- If you have to give somebody some "constructive criticism," pull them off to the side and do it one-on-one, not in front of anybody else. The old saw - "Praise in public, correct in private" – holds true in sports, at home, and in the workplace.

- Say something positive to a teammate without sounding like a dork.

2.0 Equipment

2.1 Basics

- In goal, ALWAYS wear cup, helmet, gloves, throat guard, chest protector, mouthpiece, shoes. If you normally wear glasses, use shatterproof lenses or contact lenses in goal.

- ALWAYS wear full gear in the goal or whenever somebody is shooting on you - Even if you're just "messing around," or if one of your friends says, "Hey, Joe, just hop in goal for a second – I want to show you something." This is when people get hurt. All it takes is one shot to break your windpipe or ruin your 'junk'.

- What brands of equipment are best? This booklet doesn't promote any one brand over another. There are lots of reputable companies out there. Talk to your friends and older players, try different types out, and decide for yourself what suits you best.

- Old vs. New: Don't worry about having the latest new gear – just make sure it works for you and is safe enough to protect you. You're not out there to make a "fashion statement." I've used the same stick for many, many years. In a recent game I lent my 3-year old helmet to a guy and wore my old one, which I got in 1972 – it worked just fine, I had a lot of saves, and we won the game.

Figure 2-1 – 1972 Helmet, last used in a game in April 2005
(14 saves, 5 goals allowed, we won)

2.2 Other Equipment:

Arm, shoulder, shin and/or thigh pads: Most goalies (including me) don't wear these pads because they might slow them down a little. But if you're young and need to build up some experience, and are a little worried about getting hit, there's no shame in using them. As you get older and build more confidence, you'll probably want to get rid of them.

2.3 Stick

The stick is the goalie's most important piece of equipment. There are several good brands and lots of different ways to string them. You'll have to experiment to see what suits you best. Here are a few general comments:

Shaft: The lighter the better (whatever you can afford). Some goalies use a short shaft, though I prefer the normal length, which makes it easier for me to make the long pass, and to reach up high to pick off feeds (Figure 2-2).

Figure 2-2 – Normal Length Shaft (left) and Short Shaft (right)

I put tape on my shaft, which helps my grip if it's raining (Figure 2-3).

Figure 2-3 – Tape on the Shaft

Pocket: There are a few different options to consider when you break in and set up your pocket. A deep one is good, as it helps reduce rebounds. The only possible problem is that the deep pocket might give you a whip in the stick (for newcomers, a "whip" makes the ball head lower than you want when you throw). Some goalies counteract this whip by laying the stick farther back as they wind up to throw. This can work, but takes practice.

I use a medium deep pocket, as it makes my passing more accurate and I think I can get the ball off quicker (no need for the "long windup"), which is important in a quick-clear, on-the-run, short-pass situation. Note that if I practiced more with a deeper pocket stick, I'd probably be able to throw better with it. But I've gotten so used to my current stick that I'm reluctant to change.

The negative about my stick is that the shallower pocket probably leads to more rebounds. I try to offset this with some other techniques, which I'll discuss later (e.g., soft hands, "finishing" the save completely, and angling the stick so that the rebound on a low or bounce shot drops right at my feet).

Stringing: There are several different ways to string your stick. Some people swear by the "no rebound pocket," some prefer shooting strings, some do nothing. Some like soft mesh, some like hard mesh, some swear by "normal" size mesh, others are just as adamant that "Monster Mesh" is the only way to go. I bought a stick off the shelf, broke in the pocket, never restrung it, and have been using it with good success for many years. On the other hand, my son Tom restrung his stick several times until he found what he liked best (Figure 2-4). Figures 2-4 through 2-7 show some of the options. Feel free to try any of these; practice passing, catching and saving; and eventually you'll find out what works best for you.

Figure 2-4 – "Broad V" Shooting Strings

Figure 2-5 – My Stick – "Off the rack"

Figure 2-6 – "Narrow V" shooting Strings

Figure 2-7 – "Monster" mesh (right) vs. Normal Mesh

Practice: No matter what stick you go with, the key to "having a good stick" is practice. I can't tell you how many thousands of passes I've thrown with other guys, and thousands of saves made in warm-ups, not to mention the countless hours of "wall ball" when nobody else was around.

In college, in the middle of winter, long before the season started, I used to go out almost every day and throw against the wall for at least an hour – short passes, long passes, right-handed, left-handed, overhand, three-quarters, sidearm, backhand. It was really cold, but I got better. I play left-handed in the goal, but can throw with both hands – all because of wall-ball and tossing the ball around with friends.

2.4   Equipment – Care and Feeding

Go over all your equipment carefully every day, especially the day before a game. Just the other day, I was checking my stick and noticed a crack in the wall. One day it wasn't there, but the next day it was. If I hadn't checked every day, I never would have noticed it.

Fix anything that's broken or about to break - strings, mesh, wall, straps, etc. I carry extra strings, tape, screws, and a screwdriver to every game. I also take an extra stick and cup, just in case.

3.0 Focus

So far…we've got you in a good positive attitude, and you've put on all your gear – ready to play. Now let's get your head in even better shape for jumping in between the pipes, making some saves, and becoming a great goalie.

Figure 3-1 - FOCUS

3.1 Focus is <u>Really</u> Important

But before that first shot comes at you, there's one more mental habit you need to get into. I'll summarize it with one word: FOCUS.

- In practice, while warming up or in a game, FOCUS all your attention on what's going on. Don't let your mind wander into thinking about anything else – a comment somebody made earlier in the day, your date last weekend, the movie you saw.

- This doesn't mean that you have to be uptight – in fact, you'll probably play worse if you're too tense. BUT it does mean that you are training your mind to "be in the game," not somewhere else.
  I remember one goalie in summer league who used to sing all the time. I could never figure out how he could be concentrating on both the game and the lyrics to *Satisfaction*. Well, he often seemed to react slowly to situations and never got very good. The moral of the story: When you're in the goal, focus on being a goalie, nothing else. You can work on your rock star career some other time.

- Practicing focus will help you with other parts of your game, such as:
  - Watching the ball
  - Being in the right position for a shot
  - Being in the right stance
  - Passing

One more time: Always pay attention and be ready.

The picture below gives an example of Focus: Within 5 feet of the goalie, there's just been a collision on the crease; two defenders and attackman are on the ground; a defensive middie is still in the crease; an attacker still has the ball out front. In spite of the collision, the bodies strewn around, and the people running by, the goalie is still focused on the man with the ball.

Figure 3-2 – Keep your focus – no matter what else is going on around you

3.2   Focus - Drills

A lacrosse game lasts from 90 minutes to 2 hours, and as goalie you'll need to be focused on the game-play the whole time.

- If you have a short attention span or can't concentrate for a full practice or game, then you might have Attention Deficit Disorder (ADD) or some similar condition. If so, then I'll leave the treatment to your parents, yourself, and the medical profession.

- If, however, you don't seem to have any clinical problem, then I think you can build up your ability to focus for a full game by doing things that require your full attention, for gradually longer blocks of time, over a period of several weeks. The activities would ideally engage your mind, body or both.

- I haven't done any studies that show what activities work best, but here are some things that have worked for me:

  - Mind: Reading books, and really focusing on what I'm reading about, not with the TV that's showing music videos in the background, the traffic going by, etc. Listen to music (really listen) while not doing other things. Take up a craft anything that requires you to focus intently for an hour or two. Depending on your interests, you can try carpentry, painting, building models, even Lego for younger kids.

  - Body: Any cardio exercise (running, swimming, bike, etc.). This may sound simple, but if you run or bike for a half hour or so, you'll be building up your ability to focus on something for an extended period of time. Or try any sport or game involving hand-eye coordination, like ping-pong, air hockey, or foosball. Note that it's difficult to keep your mind focused for a whole game if your body isn't in good shape.

  - Visualization: A lot has been written and discussed about athletes who visualize doing their sport – or some aspect of their sport – successfully. There are a lot of claims that this will really help to improve your game. I've tried this off and on, and I think it helps – but only if it goes along with a lot of dedicated physical and mental practice. In other words, you're not going to get much better just by imagining that you're great – you still have to put in the hours on the practice field.

4.0 Watch the BALL

This might seem like the most obvious thing to do, but I'd bet that not watching the ball is the leading mistake that goalies make. As you practice focusing on really "being in the game," the most important part of this focusing is keeping your eye on the ball.

Even the best goalies can't stop every shot. Goals are usually the result of a defensive breakdown or a great move and shot by an attacker. However, a lot of shots go in that the goalie could have – and should have – stopped. The graph below isn't based on scientific evidence, but gives my estimate of what goalie mistakes lead to the most goals. You'll notice that "Not Watching the Ball" is at the top of the list.

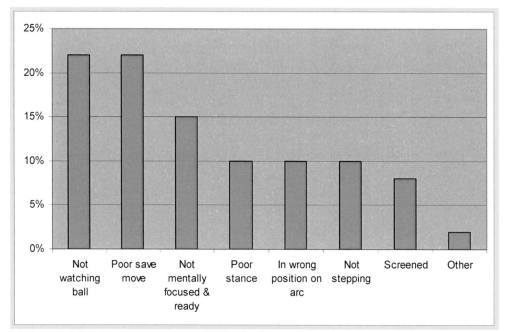

Figure 4-1 – Estimated Causes of Goals that the Goalie should have saved
(or, more accurately, estimated cause of goals scored on me, that I should saved)

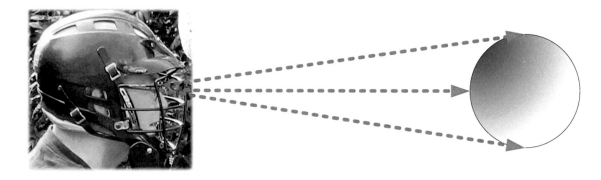

Figure 4-2 – KEEP YOUR EYE ON THE BALL!!!

4.1 Basics

In the photo below, the attacker on the left is just releasing his shot, and the goalie is looking right at the ball as it leaves the stickhead. His head is up and he's been following the ball closely as it's been passed around. When the shooter steps to fire, the goalie is ready – because he's been focusing on the ball.

Figure 4-3 – Watching the Ball

In the next photo, the goalie is again focused on the ball, in spite of the sun. On sunny days, it's a good idea to wear eye black, which helps a little. Also, shooters will shoot "out of the sun," so before the game, figure out what spots on the field will cause the most problems and set up a code word that will tell your defensemen: "Hey, the guy can shoot out of the sun now. I can't see the ball. Move him over or start playing him tighter so he can't wind up and fire."

(While I'm on the subject of the sun, before an afternoon game (especially late afternoon), it's a good idea to figure out where the sun will be in each quarter, particularly the fourth, when the sun is often getting down near the horizon. Ideally, you want this low-in-the-sky sun to be in the opponent's goalie's eyes in the last quarter – not in <u>your</u> eyes. Talk about this with your coach and captains before the game, so that they can choose the best goal to defend in the first quarter – if they have the choice. A lot of times, the sun won't be a factor for the first three periods, but will be murder at the end.)

Figure 4-4 – Watching the Ball

Here are a few things to help you watch the ball better:

- Keep your head still: Try running after a fly ball in baseball. You'll notice that if your head bobs as you run, the ball will jump around. The same thing is true in playing goalie. Your vision will be better if you can hold your head still. This is sometimes hard when the ball is being passed around quickly and you're moving from one position on the arc to another. And you don't want to stand there stiff as a board. But the point is that you don't want to bob your head around a lot, and keeping it still will improve your ability to pick up the shot.

- The ball "cues" your "save move": The instant the ball leaves the stick is when your "save move" has to start. You need to practice so that you make the right move automatically, the very instant that your eyes can detect what the path of the ball will be. We'll get into the "save moves" later on – you have to master them, but also initiate the move as fast as possible. If you don't pick up the ball

26

until it's half way – or even a quarter of the way – to the goal, then you've already lost valuable 100ths of a second.

- <u>You can't stop what you don't see:</u> One thing is sure – if you don't watch and see the ball, you won't make the save (unless you get lucky and it hits you).

- <u>Fakes:</u> Good shooters can fake with their heads, arms, hips, hands – you name it. If you fall for the fake and go one way, you can be sure that a decent shooter will aim the other way.
Preparing for and dealing with fakes is one area where learning about your opponent before the game will really help. By scouting ahead of time, I've often been able to pick out attackmen who – when they have a shot on the crease - *always* fake high and shoot low. Because I knew this before the game, I didn't fall for the high fake, and was ready to make the save down low.
BUT, regardless of how well I've scouted for fakes, **I still have to WATCH THE BALL.**

- <u>Tendencies:</u> It's true that if you're a fairly advanced goalie, you can study film of an opponent and learn about his tendencies, so that you might be able to gain a fraction of a second by noticing, for example, that before he shoots a low shot, he always goes sidearm instead of straight overhead. If you know about that tendency, then you can "cheat" a little by preparing yourself for a low shot, even before the ball leaves the stick.
But even if you know tendencies and can anticipate where a shot will go, **you still have to watch the ball.**

In the photo below, you can see that the goalie's eyes are lasered right in on the ball as he's making the save. Watching the ball all the way into the mesh is a good habit to get into, especially if you're fairly new to the game.

Figure 4-5 – Watching the Ball All the Way into the Mesh

Finally, while we're talking about watching the ball…if you don't make a clean save, do your best to figure out where the ball went. I'll talk about rebounds more in *Section 6.3.2 - The Uncontrolled Save - Rebounds.*

4.2 Drills

Here are a few things you can do to improve your ability to always be in the habit of watching the ball:

- As a fan: Go to a game as a fan and spend the whole time watching the ball closely, even when it rolls out of bounds. This trains your eyes to follow the ball, no matter where and how fast it's going: high, low, fast, slow, bouncing, rolling, passes, shots, loose balls.

- Warm-up: At practice, when warming up, REALLY FOCUS on keeping your head still, watching the ball, and reacting into your save move instantly. This is where you're starting to train yourself into these key habits. Our goal: At the instant the ball leaves the shooter's stickhead, this "cues" you into the right save move.

- At practice: During an entire scrimmage – watch the ball everywhere it goes, not just when a shooter is winding up. Watch it even at the far end of the field, when

28

it's on the ground, and, of course, especially as the opponent's offense moves it around.

- <u>In the game:</u> By this time, when you get to game-time, do the same thing: WATCH THE BALL!

- <u>Building good habits:</u> By doing this all the time, you're training yourself into a great habit that will help you make more saves than anything else you can do.

- <u>Visit an optometrist:</u> I'm not here to tell you to spend money, but an annual eye checkup is a good idea. Wearing glasses in the goal isn't bad – I've done it for over 40 years.

- <u>Eye exercises:</u> There are websites that promise great results with various eye exercises. Some major league baseball players swear by these for improving their hitting, so it's worth a look. My purpose isn't to promote one over another, so I suggest you check them out, try some of the exercises, and see how they work. My personal experience is that any hand-eye coordination activity (another sport, ping-pong, drums, air hockey, etc.) will keep your eyes sharp.

5.0 Stance

To stop a shot going 80 or 90 miles an hour, your body has to be in the right stance because the stance is the "launchpad" that you make your save move from.

5.1 Don'ts

- First, let's talk about some "don'ts," as these cover the most common mistakes:

    1) <u>Don't stand "back on your heels":</u> Be on your toes / balls of your feet.

    In the photo below, the goalie (just to our right of the cage) has his butt down and his weight on his heels. This will make it harder for him to step to the ball and react quickly if an attacker (white jerseys) picks up the loose ball and flicks a quick shot.

Figure 5-1 – Don't Sit Back on Your Heels

Figure 5-2 – Same Goalie, flat-footed

Comment: I don't mean to pick on this goalie, as I'm sure that many goalies sit back on their heels from time to time. But this is an example of a goalie who appears to have developed a bad habit that can be fixed with some direction and practice.

2) <u>Don't "dance" – no "happy feet"</u>: I can guarantee you that a good shooter will catch you in "mid-dance-step" – by the time you put that foot down and start to step, it's too late. Stay on your toes, ready to step to the ball. In general, you move your feet only to move along the arc and when you step to the ball to make the save.

3) <u>Don't stand up too straight:</u> Knees should be bent.

4) <u>Don't crouch down too low:</u> If you're too low, you give away the high shot too easily.

5) <u>Loose Arms:</u> Don't have your arms "pinned in" too close to your sides. This limits your ability to get the stick to the ball.

5.2   The Right Stance

After all those "don'ts," let's move on to the right stance. Frankly, this varies from goalie to goalie. But there are a few general principles that hold true for almost every keeper. As you get more experience and learn what works best for you, you can vary these somewhat.

In summary, you want to be in that "athletic stance" that all coaches in every sport talk about: On your toes / balls of your feet, well-balanced, knees bent a little, back fairly straight, butt down a little, head up, facing out. Ready to step to the ball and move your stick to make the save.

The two photos below show a front and side view of a pretty good basic stance.

Figure 5-3 – Basic Stance – Front View Of Right-hander   **Figure 5-4 – Basic Stance – Front View Of Left-hander**

Note: This is the same photo: I play lefty in the goal, so Figure 5-4 is the original shot. I just inverted the first shot to show what a righty would look like.
Comments: Some goalies prefer a wider stance, but I usually keep my feet at about shoulder width.

Figure 5-5 – Basic Stance -
Side View of a Right-hander
from the right side

Figure 5-6 – Basic Stance -
Side View of a Left-hander
from the left side

<u>Note:</u> *yes, this is the same photo, inverted.*
<u>Comments on this stance:</u> *As a shooter winds up, I'll lean forward just a little more, with weight on my toes / balls of the feet. Some goalies will hold the stick a little more vertically than what you see in this picture.*

If you're new to lacrosse but have played other sports, the stance is similar to defending in basketball, being "on your feet" in wrestling, linebacker in football, and infielder in baseball. But as a goalie, there are a few differences – for example, you have to figure out what to do with the stick.

When checking my stance, I like to start at the feet and work my way up – that way I can make sure that I don't forget anything. After enough practice and training yourself, you should drop into your stance without giving it a second thought – but even after a couple years, at the beginning of the day, it's a good idea to run through the "feet to head" checklist. I still do it at the beginning of every game. Look at Figures 5-3 through 5-6 above as I run through this list:

- Feet: About shoulder width apart. Toes pointed straight out or slightly pigeon-toed.

- <u>Knees, Legs:</u> Knees bent but not bent so far that you're in a deep crouch.

- <u>Waist & Back:</u> Back is fairly straight. Bend forward at the waist

- <u>Arms & Elbows:</u> Out from the body a bit. Not clamped in close to the body.

- <u>Hands:</u> Top hand right next to where the stickhead meets the shaft. Top hand grip is mainly with thumb, index and middle fingers. Bottom hand about 16 – 20 inches down the shaft from top hand. From the side, the bottom hand is farther out from the body than the top hand.

- <u>Head:</u> Head up, looking straight out at the ballhandler.

- <u>Where to position the stick head (high, low or medium):</u> See Figures 5-3 and 5-4 (above), and especially note that I'm showing as much "mesh" as I can to the shooter, i.e., I don't turn the stickhead at an angle to the shooter. Basic stickhead position covers the most area possible between the helmet and the stick-side shoulder.

  Top edge of stickhead is as high as, or a little higher than, the top pipe of the goal. The exception to this is very young goalies who are too short to keep their stickhead even with the top of the goal without reaching way out. In this case, the short goalie can just get in a normal stance with the top edge of his stickhead a few inches above the top of his helmet. If the shooter aims high, then the goalie will just have to go up for it.

Figure 5-7 – Good Stance

Comments:

- *Head up and Eyes watching ball; well balanced; stick almost vertical but covering top corner; left hand a little farther from body than right hand; arms, elbows and hands not too close to body; bent slightly at waist.*
- *Possible suggestions: Bend knees just a little more. Have feet 3" - 4" closer together. Point toes straight out at shooter. Move stick about 3" higher to be even with top pipe of goal.*
- *BTW, he made the save.*

5.2.1 Feet

- <u>Width of stance:</u> I put my feet about shoulder width apart, and this is a good place to start. Some goalies favor a really wide stance. That's ok if it works for them, but I don't recommend starting there. See how well you do with a shoulder-width stance and then experiment. I will say that I've never seen a successful goalie who keeps his feet really close together.

- <u>Toes:</u> You need to be on the balls of your feet. I try to find the exact point where I'm not falling forward, but am a) definitely not back on my heels, and b) balanced on that area of the foot that I can push off fastest from. Try to find this spot by checking out different foot placements and weight adjustments. Trust me – the right spot is there, but you have to spend some time looking for it.

- <u>Where to point your toes:</u> Controversial area here. If you're new to goalie, I suggest you just point your toes more or less straight ahead or a little pigeon-toed. I usually stand very slightly pigeon-toed, and it seems to make my step just an instant quicker, and gives that step a little extra drive. But it might be different for you, so just try it and see if it works. Just for the heck of it, I've even tried standing splay-footed (toes pointed out), but I found this slows down my first step.

However, I've seen some goalies, even at the Major League Lacrosse level, who point their toes out a little. This may be because at that level, the shots are so fast that there's often no time to take a full step - but by having the toes pointed outward, it's easier to keep your balance and control the stickhead when you can't take a full step but at least can move your weight toward the line of the shot. But, to me anyway, this is an advanced technique that can be left to the pros. Until you're playing for the Bayhawks, I recommend avoiding the "splay-footed" stance.

Figure 5-8 – Toes Straight Ahead – Works for many goalies

Figure 5-9 – Splay-Footed: Not best for new goalies, but a few people use it.

Figure 5-10 – Slightly Pigeon-Toed – Works best for me

Figure 5-11 – More Pigeon-Toed – recommended by some goalies and coaches

- <u>Weight on toes:</u> Weight needs to be evenly balanced between the left and right feet, because you don't know whether you'll have to step to the right or the left. Most of us are right-handed and therefore right-footed, so we might tend to put a little more weight on that foot, and thus be able to push off our right foot a bit quicker. The problem with this is when you're right-handed and you need to step to a shot on the stick side. I've noticed that, contrary to what you might think, many goalies have a hard time with stick side shots, especially low ones. Being right-footed, in their pre-shot stance, they put more weight on the right foot. So when a shot comes stick-side low, they have to shift that weight over to the left foot, which they then have to push off from in order to take that first step to the right. All this takes only a few 100ths of a second, but it's often enough to make you late to the shot.

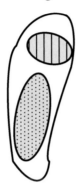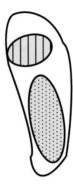

*Figure 5-12 – Weight on Balls of the Feet (vertical lined-ellipse). **NOT on the heels or arch (dotted ellipse)***

As goalie, you have to step equally fast in both directions, so you have to train yourself to balance your weight evenly between your two feet. This takes practice.

The drill I still use is simple, and you can do it anywhere, any time: Just take your stick, get in your stance, balance the weight, then practice stepping to the right, first slowly, then gradually faster and faster. Do that 10 times to the right, then 10 to the left, first for high shots, then hip, then low. Repeat often!

Some people recommend a drill called 'walking the line' or something similar. The 'walking the line' means that you just do your stepping up and down the sideline.

Whether outdoors or in, just remember to get set in your full, pre-shot stance before each step. I'll talk more about Stepping to the Ball in Section 7.0.

5.2.2 Knees

As noted above, don't stand straight up and don't bend over too far. Bend your knees and find out a) where you're comfortable, and b) how much bend gives you the fastest, most explosive first step. The knee bend works closely with balancing on the balls of your feet; that means that you need to find a position where the knees are bent some <u>and</u> your balance is good, ready to spring forward.

Figure 5-13 – Keep your knees bent
Comments: Knees bent. Left foot will come down and get set before shooter winds up.

Figure 5-14 – Good Stance
Comments: Very good basic stance. Note bent knees. Toes might be pointed out a little too much.

<u>Possible Exceptions:</u> There may be a couple of exceptions to this basic approach to bending the knees. For example, if a guy is winding up sidearm or underarm from outside, or if I know that a guy almost always shoots low, then I'll usually crouch down

just a bit lower. In my case, this seems to give me a better look at a shot that comes from sidearm or underhand, and it brings me down a little closer to the low shot.

Of course, some guys shoot high from sidearm, but the good news is that if my knees are bent just a bit more than usual, and he shoots high, then I can usually step and spring up at the ball pretty quickly, because – for me anyway - when the leg is bent a bit more, the quads can give a stronger contraction and "pop" me up toward the ball.

5.2.3 Waist and Back

If your feet, knees and head are in the right positions, and you straighten your back, you should be fine. When I say the back is "straight," I don't mean straight and stiff – but just so it's not curled way over.

Figure 5-15 – Waist and Back
Comments: Keeping the back fairly straight, but leaning forward from the waist helps to keep weight on the toes and balls of the feet, ready to step out to the ball.

5.2.4 Hands

Hand placement on the stick is important. It may seem obvious, but there are lots of ways to do it wrong, which will slow down your save move and make it harder to control the ball on the save. Here are a few things to think about as you grab hold of the pole.

- Top Hand: I recommend holding your top hand (i.e., your right hand if you're right-handed) just below where the head attaches to the stick. Some people like to hold the bottom part of the stickhead (the sort of triangular-shaped part), as they feel this gives them better control. You can try this and see if it works for you.

   Top Hand Grip: With your top hand, don't grip the shaft like it's a baseball bat, i.e., with all four fingers and your thumb curled around it. I hold the stick mainly with my thumb, index and middle fingers. This allows for more flexibility and speed as I make my save moves.

Figure 5-16 – Top Hand Grip
Note that this isn't a "four-finger, full-fist, baseball bat grip." I control the "top" of the stick mainly with my index and middle fingers, plus the thumb.

- "Sighting": Some coaches recommend "sighting" at the ball by using thumb on the top hand as a kind of rifle sight and keeping it "aimed" at the ball before the shot is released. Some people swear by this method and claim good results.

   I practiced this technique a few times and think it works pretty well when the ballhandler is carrying his stickhead relatively high, anywhere above his shoulder. My only problem was trying to use it when the shooter's stickhead goes sidearm or low – at that point trying to "aim" with my thumb seemed to pull me out of position – it pulls my stickhead lower than I normally carry it, and seemed to throw my balance off a little, i.e., left me leaning over to my stick-side more than I like. Maybe I just need to practice it more. Since many people like it, I recommend that you give it a try and see if it works for you. You'll probably need help from a coach who's better versed in this technique than I am. The main point I take away is that whatever you do, you have to watch the ball, with or without aiming your thumb.

- <u>Bottom Hand:</u> When in the stance, ready for a shot, I have my bottom hand about 16" – 18" from my top hand. But note that I have fairly short arms, so this distance will probably be different for you. I've seen a few decent goalies who keep the hands much farther apart than 18" or really close together (12") – this might work for you, but I don't advise starting with it. Both "real close" and "real far" can interfere with your mechanics. For example, take the "really far" grip and then try to stop an offside low shot.

Figure 5-17 – Distance between Hands
Short goalie (5' 8"): Hands about 16" apart

Figure 5-18 – Distance between Hands
Taller goalie (5' 10"): Hands about 18" – 20" apart

5.2.5 Arms & Elbows

- First, to review the "Don't": Don't have your arms, elbows and hands really close to the body. To test this out, take your normal stance, but with hands close to your chest and elbows tucked in close to your sides. Then have a guy shoot an offside low shot. 99.9% of the time, you just can't get to it in time because your body is in the way of the arms and hands.

- I keep my elbows bent and lifted up slightly from my sides. With this approach, I never get "handcuffed" by having the arms and hands too close. See Figure 5-19 below:

Figure 5-19 – Basic Stance - Side View of a Right-hander from the right side

Comments: Note arms, elbows and hands are away from the body. "Bottom" (left) hand is farther out from body than right hand.
Note: Since I'm a lefty, I inverted this photo to give this view of a righty.

- <u>Amount of elbow bend:</u> But…some goalies like to keep their arms out almost straight. If that works for them, fine, but I don't recommend starting out with it.

- <u>View from the side – lower hand farther out:</u> I always have my bottom (lower) hand out a bit farther than top (upper) hand (see Figure 5-19 above). This makes it easier for me to get to the offside shots. Also, when I move the stick to the save, it keeps the full area of the stick facing the shot. When you move your stick to make a save, if the head is slanted (i.e., the butt end of the stick is farther back toward to the goal than the head), then a) you're not presenting the most "saving area" possible to the ball, and b) even if the ball hits the mesh or head, it can glance off and directly into the goal.

Figure 5-20 – "Bottom" hand (left hand for a right-hander) is farther out from body than top hand

- <u>Hand position – for low shots:</u> Having the bottom hand farther out than the top is especially important on bounce and low shots. If you don't make a clean save, but the ball hits the mesh or head, then that bottom hand will have brought the stick to a position where it head "aims" the rebound right at the ground, not up and not straight out in front of the goal.
See Figures 5-21 and 5-22 below: This shows where the stick starts and where it ends up if my stick starts out in the right position. I kind of "spin" the stick down like a propeller, i.e., on the same 'plane' when viewed from the side.

Figure 5-21 – Stance – Bottom hand is farther out so that on low and bounce shots, when I snap the stickhead down to make the save…(see Figure 5-22 below….

Figure 5-22 – …the stick will be angled so that the rebound will drop at my feet

- <u>View from the front – stickhead position:</u> Looking from the front, this is some controversy about where to hold the stickhead. Some goalies hold the shaft vertical or almost completely vertical. Others like it over to the side. I hold mine almost straight up and down, but angled a bit to the left (I'm left-handed), right next to my head. This means that my face covers the goal in case of a "center high" shot, my stick covers most of the stick-side high shot, and my stick doesn't have that far to go for the offside high shot. See Figure 5-23 below:

Figure 5-23 – Good Stickhead Position

- <u>Stickhead Position – What not to do:</u>
  - If you have the stick right in front of your face, then you won't be covering some of the stick-side high area.
  - If you have it too far over toward the stick-side (i.e., angled pretty far from vertical), then you'll have farther to go to get the offside high shot. For example, in Figure 5-23 above, if I lowered my left hand farther down, then: (a) the stickhead would be too low to deal with the stick-side high shot, and (b) the stickhead would have too far to go to reach the offside high shot.

Figure 5-24 – Shaft Position

Comments: Note that shaft is almost vertical, when viewed from the front. Top edge of stickhead is about even with the top edge of the goal.

You have to experiment and see what works for you, but to start with, I recommend keeping the stick almost vertical, but with the stickhead just to the side of your face.

5.2.6 Head

We've worked our way up from the feet and finally reached the head. As mentioned in Sections 4.0 and 5.0, keep your head up, looking out at the ball. Also, try to keep it fairly still, not bobbing around, as this will make it easier to pick up the ball coming off the shooter's stickhead. Make sure the bars of your facemask don't obscure your view. If a bar is cutting across your field of vision, adjust your helmet straps until you have a clear view.

6.0 Position & Moving on the Arc

OK, to recap: we've got you going with your great positive attitude, good equipment, focusing on the task at hand, watching the ball, and standing there in a perfect stance, ready to pounce.

6.1 The Arcs

Next question is: When the ball is out front or behind, where the heck do I stand? Once again, there are choices and raging controversies in the goalie and coaching community.

- There are 3 basic "arcs" to choose from: flat, medium, and high (see Figure 6-1). Each has some pros and cons:

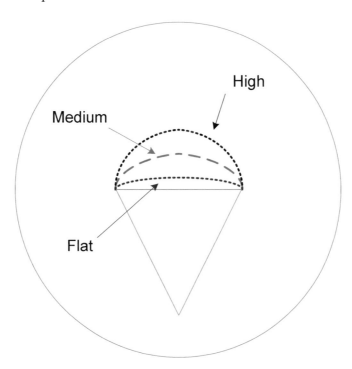

Figure 6-1 – The Arcs

Note: In this diagram, the lines representing the 3 arcs aren't meant to be the exact distances from the goal line that a goalie stands when playing a flat, medium or high arc. For example, a high arc might be even farther out: I'll discuss this more below.

The photos below show the general spot where a goalie stands on the flat, medium and high arcs. The "Notes" below each picture are meant to indicate that there is no single spot that defines each arc, and that there's some flexibility as to where a goalie stands on each arc. You can experiment with different positions and see what works best for you.

Figure 6-2 – Flat Arc

Note: A goalie using a flat arc could stand even farther back than the goalie in this picture, up to the point where the heels are almost on the goal-line. Trevor Tierney, one of the best goalies in the game today, plays a flat arc. Note that this goalie holds his bottom hand farther out than some.

Figure 6-3 – Medium Arc

Note: A goalie using a medium arc could stand even farther back than the goalie in this picture. I normally play a medium or medium/flat arc, and stand about 6 - 12 inches farther back than this goalie.

Figure 6-4 – Very High Arc

Note: This goalie is on a very high arc. A standing about a foot farther back would still be on a high arc.

Following are some more detailed comments about each arc:

1) **Flat:** A completely flat arc would mean that you stand with your heels just barely in front of the goal line. But standing with you heels 12" to 18" from the goal line can also be considered a flat arc.
    a. Pros:
        i. Since you're a little farther from the shooter, you have a little more time to react to the shot.
        ii. It's easier and faster to go from the right pipe to the far left pipe (or vice versa), when a feed goes across the field.
        iii. Should make it easier to stop backside cutters coming around the corner, because if you're on a flat arc, you're obviously closer to the pipe than if you're, say, way out on a high arc.

    b. Cons:
        i. You aren't cutting down the shooter's angle at all and are giving him a lot of open net to shoot at.
        ii. If you get a piece of a shot and it dribbles behind you, it's in the goal.
        iii. If the ball is at Top Right or Top Left, or Right or Left Pipe, you're so far back that you have less chance of intercepting any passes that go across the goal mouth.

Figure 6-5 – Flat Arc

Figure 6-6 – Flat Arc

2) **High:** A high arc means that you still keep to the pipes when the ball is at or near GLE, but stand farther out toward the shooter when the ball is anywhere other than on the pipe.
   a. Pros:
      i. Cuts down the angle.
      ii. Often easier to "snuff" a bounce shot before it takes a bad hop.
      iii. If the opponent is doing a lot of cutting right on the crease, you will sometimes (depending on where the feed is coming from) be closer to the shooter, which might make it easier for you to stuff him.
      iv. Gives you a chance to stop the "dribblers" before they reach the goal.

   b. Cons:
      i. Gives you less time to react, since you're closer to the shooter.
      ii. Opens up the backside, making it easier for an opponent to cut behind you off the corners.
      iii. If you're fairly new to the game, the high arc makes it easier for you to get "lost", i.e., not knowing a) if you're giving up too much open net on one side or the other, and b) where the pipe is, in case you have to get back.

Figure 6-7 – Very High Arc

3) **Medium:** This arc places you about halfway between the flat and the high arc.
   a. Pros and Cons:
      i. More time to react than high arc, but less than flat arc.
      ii. Easier to get "lost" than flat arc but harder than high arc.
      iii. Open to backside, but not as bad as high arc.
      iv. Cuts down on most "dribblers."

Figure 6-8 – Medium Arc

Flat vs. Medium vs. High Arc: What really happens

So, does a high arc really give a goalie all that much benefit, by cutting down the angle and making the goal smaller? Or is a flat arc better because it gives him more time to react? The longer you play goalie, the more arguments you'll hear about this. I've already covered some pros and cons of each arc. Now I'll look at the debate from a mathematical perspective, and then make some recommendations.

First, let's look at what a shooter's-eye view of a goalie on a flat vs. a high arc:

Figure 6-9 – Flat Arc – What the Shooter Sees

Figure 6-10 – High Arc – What the Shooter Sees

Note: Because the goalie in Figure 6-10 has come out toward the shooter from where he was in Figure 6-9, the goal is now "smaller," as now represented by the black dotted lines. This is what happens when you cut down the angle by playing a higher arc. But, of course, the goalie has less time to react to the shot.

Higher Math: If you prefer a mathematical approach to all this, here are some figures to think about:

- The goal is 6' by 6', so the goalie has to cover 36 square feet, or 5,184 square inches.
- If I assume an average goalie size of 5' 9" tall and medium build, his body and stick will cover a total area of about 8.625 square feet, or 1,242 square inches.
- If the goalie stands right on the goal line, that leaves 27.375 square feet – or 3,942 square inches – uncovered.

The following assumes a shot coming from 30 feet away:
For every foot the goalie moves out from the goal line, he reduces the total area he has to cover by about 1.15 square feet, or about 165 square inches.

However, for every foot he comes out, he loses about $8/1000^{th}$ of a second to react – on a 90 mph shot. This might not seem like much, but that's almost $1/100^{th}$ of a second. A 90 mph shot from 30 feet takes only 0.227 second to go 30 feet.

So when the goalie moves out from the goal line (30 feet from the shooter) to a higher arc (26 feet from the shooter, i.e., 4 feet off the goal line), two things happen:

1) The goalie has less area to cover – 4,516 square inches when 4 feet out from the goal line, versus 5,184 square inches when right on the goal line – a difference of 668 square inches), **BUT**
2) The goalie has less time to react - 0.197 second for the ball to go 26 feet versus 0.227 second to go 30 feet – a difference of 0.03 second.

In summary, when out on the high arc, the amount of area he has to cover has been reduced by about 4.6 square feet, or 12.9%,
BUT the time he has to react has also decreased – by about 3/100ths of a second or about 13.3%.

All of which means to me that there is no easy, mathematical proof that the high, medium or flat arc is best. In light of all this, plus my own experience in playing and watching other goalies, my recommendations are below:

A couple of suggestions:

1) Start with a Medium/Flat or Medium Arc: When you first start in the goal, I recommend a medium or medium/flat arc. This means that when the ball is at Top Center, you stand with your heels about 20" to 28" from the goal line.

2) <u>Adjusting based on experience:</u> As you gain experience, you can change your arc to best suit your own strengths and weaknesses.
   a) For example, if you have great reflexes, but your lateral motion is not so great, you might want to play a higher arc: With those super reflexes of yours, being a bit closer to the shooter won't hurt you much, plus the narrower angle decreases the lateral area you have to cover.
   b) But if the opposite is true – great lateral movement, but maybe not the greatest reflexes - you might do better from a flatter arc. By being farther from the shooter, you obviously give yourself more time to react to the shot.
   c) If you have both great reflexes and speedy lateral movement, then you can play a flat or medium/flat arc – this will maximize the time you have to react (always a plus, no matter how quick you are), you'll be able to save those nasty shots into the low far corner, and you'll be able to guard against backdoor cutters.

3) <u>Mix it up:</u> As you gain even more experience, you'll find that each arc can be best for a certain game situation.
   a) <u>Backdoor?:</u> For example, if the opponent is known for trying the backdoor cut, then I play a medium-to-flat arc so I can cover the backside better.
   b) <u>Bounce shots from outside?:</u> But if they normally just pass to an open middie, who then cranks bounce shots from outside, I'll go out onto a medium arc to cut down his angle and be in better position to 'snuff' the bounce shots.
   c) <u>High hard ones from outside?:</u> On the other hand if a certain middie has a real cannon, when he has the ball, I'll usually drop back into a flatter arc to give myself just a bit more time to react.

4) <u>My approach:</u> I seldom play a really high arc, as I have pretty good lateral movement and decent reflexes - hanging in a medium to medium-flat arc gives me every last 1000th of a second I can get to react and make the save.

5) <u>Your approach:</u> But my "arc play" isn't guaranteed best for everybody. Try the different arcs in different situations, get feedback from your coach and teammates in warm-up, and eventually you'll find out what works best for you.

6.2   Position & Moving on the Arc

Now that we know where the arcs are, we have to figure out where to stand on the imaginary line of the arc.

In summary, it's pretty simple: You stand in the spot that cuts down the shooter's angle most, and doesn't provide too much empty net on either side of you.

(The exception to this is when you're trying to tempt a guy to shoot in a certain place, one of the spots that you know you can get to fast. See *Section 16.0 – Temptation* for more details, but in summary: Let's say you're really quick at getting to offside low shots, and you want to "tempt" the shooter to aim there. So you stand so that a lot of empty net shows when he looks at that spot. He then shoots offside low, but you have a great move there and make the save. Some goalies refer to this trick as "baiting." It's an extremely effective technique that I've used for many years, usually with great success.)

6.2.1 Some Diagrams and Photos that Show Positioning

See Figures 6-11 through 6-23 below for diagrams and photos of where to stand on the arc.

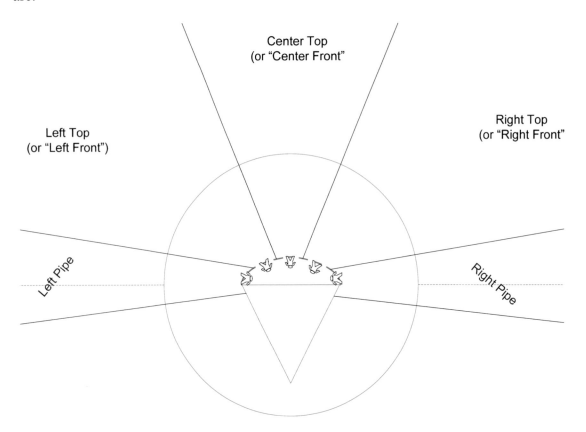

Figure 6-11 – Goalie's Position on the Arc Depends on Ball Location
Note: Some goalies say "Front" instead of "Top": Either is fine, as long as your defense knows what you mean.

As the ball moves from Right Pipe, to Right Top, to Center Top, to Left Top, to Left Pipe the goalie moves on the arc to keep the angle cut down as much as possible, and not leave either side of the net more open than the other. Figure 6-11 above shows the approximate spots where the goalie stands for different ball locations.

The diagrams and photos below cover each of the main ball locations and where to stand:

1) Ball Right Pipe

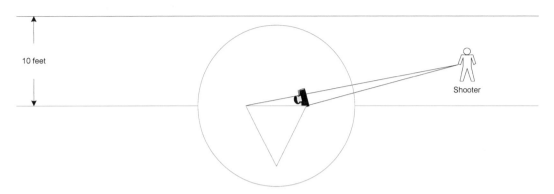

10 feet

Shooter

Figure 6-12 – Ball Right Pipe

Figure 6-13 – Ball Right Pipe
(Note: Don't be thrown off by Tom suddenly being a left-hander – Just inverted the photo.)

Figure 6-14 – Ball Moving from Right Pipe to Top Right.
Note: Goalie comes off the pipe a few inches, but still needs to watch for shot at the inside pipe (that small sliver of open net between his right side and the right pipe).

2) Ball Right Top (or "Right Front")

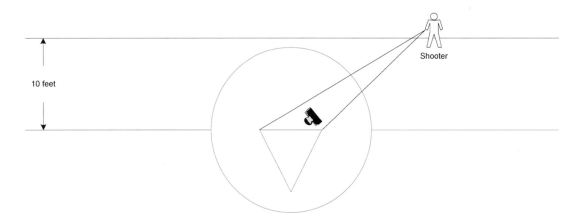

Figure 6-15 – Ball Right Top

Figure 6-16 – Ball Right Top

3) Ball Center Top (or "Center Front")

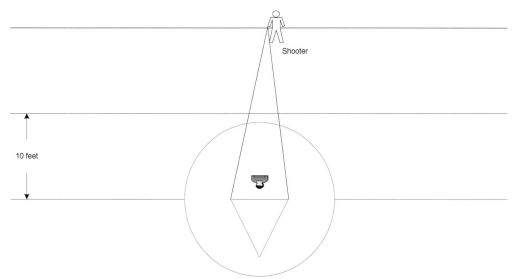

Figure 6-17 – Ball Center Top

Figure 6-18 – Ball Center Top (Medium Arc)

Comments: Note that being on a medium arc will allow the goalie to get to the back door fast if a feed goes to the attacker standing on the left crease. If the goalie were on a high arc, he'd have farther to go. If on a flat arc, he'd have less distance to go, but wouldn't be cutting down the angle on the ballhandler, if he decides to shoot.

4) Ball Left Top (or "Left Front")

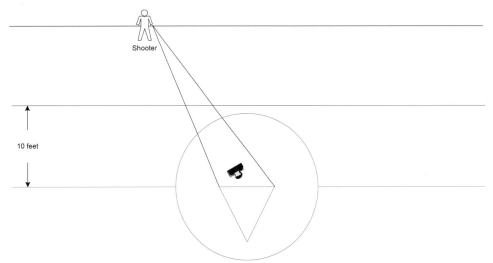

Figure 6-19 – Ball Left Top

Figure 6-20 – Ball Left Top (High Arc)

Comment: From the photographer's point of view, it looks like the goalie is leaving a lot of net open, but from the shooter's point of view, the goal is well-covered.

Figure 6-21 – Ball Left Top (Flat to Medium Arc)

5) Ball Left Pipe

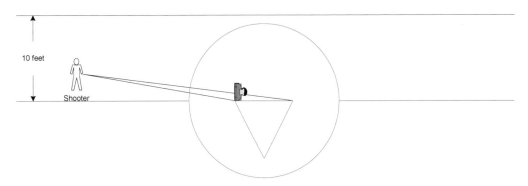

10 feet

Shooter

Figure 6-22 – Ball Left Pipe

Figure 6-23 – Ball Left Pipe

Comments: Position on the pipe shuts down any shot at the inside pipe. Note left foot right next to the pipe. This goalie is carrying his stickhead very high. I would normally carry mine lower than this, but each keeper develops his own style that works for him. A beginning goalie wants to carry the stickhead lower than this.

6.2.2 Ball Out Front

The Basics

So, to summarize the basics: Standing to cut down the angle and not giving away too much of either side of the goal seems obvious when you think about it, but it takes some practice to automatically be in the right spot without having to look back at the pipes to see where you are.

If the ballhandler is running from Right Top, to Center Top, to Left Top, the goalie just moves along the arc and gets into the best position to cut down the angle and stay in the middle of the goal, as it's seen by the shooter. This is relatively easy to master, but you need to practice it a fair amount when you're just starting in the goal. See Figure 6-24 below.

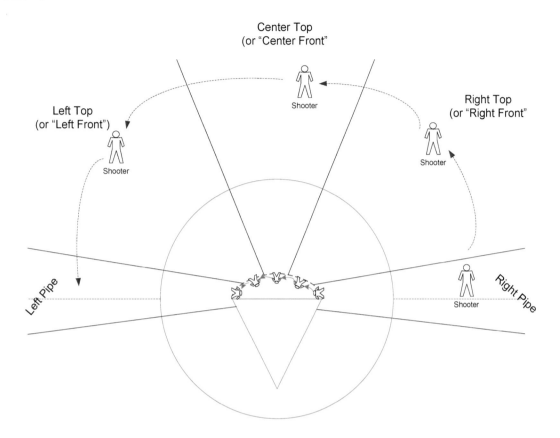

Figure 6-24 – Moving on the Arc

Comment: As the ball moves from Right Pipe, to Top Right, to Top center, and so on ("dashed" arrows), the goalie moves on his arc (small arrows) to stay in the best position for a) not giving more open goal on one side or the other, and b) cut down the shooter's angle as much as possible.

Note also that as the ball moves from spot to spot, and as I move on my arc, I want to maximize the amount of time that I'm in my "ready to save" stance, and minimize the amount of time it takes me to get from one place on the arc to the next. This means that I want to take as few steps as possible. Usually, I can use just one fast step to get from my "Ball Right Pipe" stance to my "Ball Right Top" stance. As you practice moving on the arc, make sure that your feet aren't dancing around a lot: Good shooters will fire as soon as they see that your feet are unsettled.

Positioning Drill #1: A simple drill is just to have a ballhandler run from place to place, and stop every 10 feet or so. As goalie, you move along your arc as he moves. When he stops, look down and see where you're standing to make sure you're in the best spot. Also have him tell you if you're leaving one side of the goal too open.

Positioning Drill #2: A similar drill is to have guys pass the ball from Top Left to Top Center, Top Left to Top Right, etc. As the ball is in the air, you judge where it's going to end up and go to the right spot. Check your position after each pass, and, again, have the guys out front tell you if you're in the right place.

Keeping track of your location: Here are a couple of techniques to help you know where you are on the arc:

- Tapping the pipes: When the ball is out front, I grew up touching the pipes with the head and the butt end of the stick, so that's what works for me. As long as the guy isn't winding up and a shot isn't imminent, I can take a quick tap of one pipe or the other and know where I am. I've seen one coach forbid this technique, but it's worked well for me. The only problem can come if you play a high arc and can't reach back to the pipe with your stick. If you play high, then you'll need to use other visual cues like the crease.

- Check out the crease: Glance at the crease every now and then (NOT when a shooter is winding up). This will show you how far out you are from the goal-line, and where you are in relation to the goal. If you want to be on a medium arc and look down and find the crease just 6 inches from your shoe, then obviously you've wandered too far out.

- Visual Cues: Before the game, I usually drag my spikes across the center of the crease, to make a mark that's perpendicular to the crease. This mark can be a good reference point if you get "lost" for a second. Frankly, I seldom need to look at it during a game, but it's not a bad idea, especially if you're new to the goal. Some people also make other marks that basically extend the line out from the "triangle-shaped" goalpipes on the ground. This might help you out, especially if you play a high arc. See Figure 6-25 below.
  Turf: Note that if I'm playing on artificial turf, there's obviously no dirt to drag my spikes in, so I'll usually find a leaf, small piece of paper, or short string and put it in the top middle of the crease line. The only problem is that these objects can get moved around a lot, so I have to check on the location whenever I get a chance.

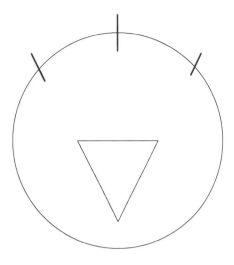

Figure 6-25 –Marks on crease – made by dragging spikes

6.2.3 Guarding the Pipe

When the ball is out front, the goalie's correct position is fairly straightforward. However, when the ball is at Left or Right Pipe, there are a few additional tricks to learn.

- Foot and stance on the pipe: If the guy with the ball is 2-3 feet behind GLE, even with GLE, or just in front of GLE, then you need to guard the pipe. In summary, when the ball is at Right Pipe, I touch the right pipe with the outside edge of my right foot and then getting into my normal stance. (Obviously, the same goes for my left foot when the ball is at Left Pipe.)

- Guard the inside pipe: What you NEVER want to do is show much space between your body and the pipe. Hitting the "inside pipe" (as this area is called) is the easiest shot for a guy coming around the corner from behind.

- When to straighten up a little: It might seem that the best way to cover the "inside pipe" is to stand up straight and have your whole left (or right) side "glued" to the pipe, thus giving the guy nothing at all to shoot at between you and the pipe. This approach can work when the shooter's angle is extremely narrow – but the problem is that that narrowness usually lasts only an instant, so when/if the shooter comes out front just a bit more, you could be stuck standing straight up, not in a good stance to make a save from, and giving him a lot of net on the far side to shoot at.

  So I often stand up straight and stay glued to the pipe only when the angle is very, very narrow (e.g., when the shooter is even with or a foot in front of GLE). But I then immediately go into my normal, "ready to save" stance as soon as the guy even looks like he's about to move farther out front, e.g., 3 feet in front of GLE.

Moving from Pipe to Pipe

Sometimes when the ballhandler is at Left Pipe and you're in position, he'll manage to sneak a pass all the way across to a cutter coming in from Right Pipe. You then have to move fast from your Left Pipe position to Right Pipe. The pictures below show how to do this quickly. Practice this move a lot - it will keep you from getting beat on the backdoor pass.

Figures 6-26 to 6-29 below show a goalie moving from Left Pipe to Right Pipe. Note that he gets there by turning clockwise. His first step is with his right foot, then to the right pipe position with his left foot, and quickly into his stance with his final step with his right foot.

Figure 6-26 – # 1: Goalie in position for Ball at Left Pipe

Figure 6-27 – # 2: As the pass goes toward a cutter at Right Pipe, goalie turns clockwise and steps with right foot. The foot goes onto the goal line or even a few inches back into the goal.

Figure 6-28 – # 3: Goalie steps with left foot, so that he'll be in the right position for ball at Right Pipe.

Figure 6-29 – # 4: Goalie steps with right foot, so that he's now in the right position for ball at Right Pipe.

#5 – Goalie will then bend knees and get into "ready to save" stance.

6.2.4 Ball Behind

When the ball is behind the goal, the goalie needs to pay close attention to being in the right place. One tendency that some goalies have is to relax a little, just because a guy can't score from behind GLE. Relaxing when the ball is behind is a bad habit to get into. In fact, your focus has to be just as intense as when the ball is out front – because only one quick pass separates "ball behind" from "shot – goal!"

To make sure you're in the right position, there are three main places to think about when the ball is behind: Center Back (also called "X"), Right Back and Left Back.

X (Center Back)
When the ball is at X, I stand in the middle of the goalmouth, about 12 to 18 inches from the goal-line. I face the ballhandler directly, but have to be ready to turn in either direction if he feeds, or to move as he moves. (More on turns and moving in a minute.) See Figure 6-30 below:

Balhandler

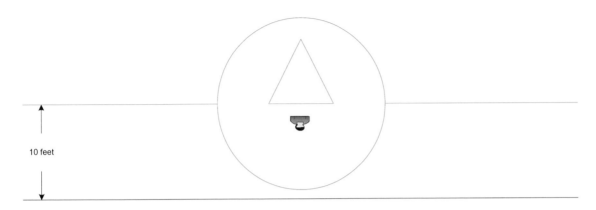

10 feet

Figure 6-30 – Ball at X: Goalie faces ballhandler

Figure 6-31 – Ball at X: Correct Position – View from X

Note: In this photo, the goalie has his stickhead just above the pipe. This is my normal approach, to help cut off passing lanes, though see note on Figure 6-32 below.

Figure 6-32 – Ball at X: Correct Position – View from Top center
Note: In this photo, the goalie has his stickhead just below the pipe. He's hoping this will lull the feeder into forgetting that the goalie can quickly reach up and intercept a feed.

- <u>Let's start with the simplest situation:</u> The attackman has the ball at X, is cradling, protecting the ball, and your D-man is keeping the guy at bay, playing "normal" defense, i.e., poke, poke, lift, poke. Since the ballhandler isn't heading hard for the pipe, that means he's probably looking for cutters to feed to.

  One question I get a lot is: Should the goalie watch the ballhandler's eyes? If the guy is really good, then the answer is "no," as even semi-decent feeders can look one way and throw another. If he's not that great, or if you've already seen in the game that he always looks where he throws, then the answer is "yes, watch his eyes," and get your stick into the passing lane he's looking at. Or tempt him to pass where he's looking by having your stickhead to the right or left of where he's looking: Then when he feeds, you'll be ready to intercept the pass.

- <u>Cutting off passing lanes:</u> Something you might want to try: If a guy is looking first one way, then another, then another, what I often do is randomly move my stickhead into different passing lanes. This makes <u>me</u> the unpredictable one.

  My rationale for doing this?: If the goalie just stands there with his stickhead in the same place all the time, then the feeder figures that out and has an easier time finding an open lane. The random movements I do aren't a wild, swinging of the stick – they are abrupt and controlled, because I still want to be able to turn and have my stick in the right place if he does get a feed past me.

I've found that this "random" approach often keeps the guy from getting a feed off, even when a cutter is open, and also gives my D-man some time to recover if he starts to get beat. Eventually, the feeder gives up and tosses the ball to the side, where they'll have to try something else.

Feeding from behind is a big part of some teams' offense, so if you can take it away from them, or make it weaker, then you've cut them off from a way they might usually score a few goals a game.

- The turn when he feeds: Now let's say that the feeder gets off a feed and you have to turn and be ready to make the save. You need to practice the turn a lot, in both directions.

  - If the ball is at X and the feed goes to the Right Top, then the goalie wants to turn in a counter-clockwise direction to get to the right spot on the arc.

  - Conversely, if the ball is at X and the feed goes to Left Top, then the goalie turns clockwise. Try this out and you'll see what I mean: If you turn the wrong way, you have farther to go, and will be slow in getting into your stance at the right place on the arc.

- The drills are simple: Have a feeder behind the goal, passing to all points in front of the goal. If you can't intercept the pass, then your job is to turn and get into the right "ready to save" stance as fast as possible. Here are a couple things to focus on when practicing the turn:

  - Stickhead Position :
    a) Stickhead High – above the bar: When the ball is behind, your stickhead is normally above the top pipe of the goal (see Figure 6-31 above), so you can try to prevent or intercept the feed. When the feed is made, as I turn I keep my stickhead at the same height as the feed. For example, if the feed is, say, 7 feet above the ground, that means that the most dangerous person will be an opponent cutting toward or right on the crease, with his stickhead also about 7 feet above the ground. If I put my stickhead at 7 feet, then when I turn, I at least have a decent chance of stuffing him or at least cutting down the shooter's angle. If my stick is at 6 feet or even 5 feet, then I obviously have less of a chance to stop the shot.

    b) Stickhead Low – below the bar: Note that some goalies will keep their stickhead low, hoping to "hide" their stick from the feeder, and snag a feed by reaching up for it as it goes over the goal (see Figure 6-

32 above). The problem with this is that if a feed is fast and high – which feeds usually are – and the goalie can't intercept it, then the goalie has to bring his stickhead up as he turns, so that he can match "stick on stick" as the shooter gets the ball and fires.

The extra time it takes to raise the stick – even if it's only a few hundredths of a second – can be the difference between a save and a goal. I don't think that "hiding" the stickhead in this way really fools many feeders: They know the goalie has a stick – it's not exactly a secret. Yes, the feeder might get careless every now and then, but not often.

c) <u>Matching the feed's height:</u> On the other hand, if the feeder is cutting from X toward Right Back, and makes a low feed, say 4 feet above ground level to a cutter coming from Right Front, then when I turn, I'll bend my knees and adjust my stick to be at about 4 feet above ground level. If I turn fast, get into my "ready to save" stance fast, and have my stick at the right level, then I should be in good position to optimize cutting down the angle and make a move on the shot. If I keep my stick high, at the 7 or so feet that it's usually at when the ball is behind, then my stickhead will be too high for a sidearm shot coming in from 3 or 4 feet above ground level.

• <u>Don't drop your stick!:</u> I've noticed that on all feeds of any heights, a lot of goalies tend to always drop their stick down when they turn. This is a really bad habit that you have to practice against. Practice your turns and getting your stickhead at the same height as the feed. See Figure 6-33 below.

Figure 6-33 – Ball is between X and Right Back –
Goalie Drops Stick: Usually a Bad Idea

- Guarding against the "Over the top" shot: When most cutters get a high feed in close, they like to shoot over the top of the goalie's stickhead. When a feed is high, and as you turn, if you see a shooter there with his arms extended so that his stickhead is fairly high, ready to catch the feed and quick-stick it, it's usually best to have your own stickhead even higher than you might think it ought to be. Several years ago, I found that guys were almost always shooting just over my stickhead, so I adjusted and now go 6 to 12 inches higher than I used to. This has led to a lot more stuffs. It doesn't always work, but give it a try, practice it, and I hope you have the same results. It may be especially good for short goalies (like me).

Ball at Right Back

Now let's move from Ball at X to a different situation, Ball Right Back. The principles are the same as when the ball is at X: If you've figured out that he passes where he looks, then watch his eyes – while still watching the ball, of course - and use this to your advantage. If he looks one way and passes somewhere else, then ignore his eyes. In either case, use your stickhead to guard the passing lanes and be ready to turn.

The main difference between X and Right Back (or Left Back) is in where you stand. As mentioned, with the ball at X, you can stand in the middle of the goal, about 12 – 18 inches off the goal-line. Figures 6-34 and 6-35 below show the correct positions when the ball is at Right Back and Left Back.

Figure 6-34 – Ball Right Back – Good Position: ready to get to the Right Pipe if attackman heads for that corner, or go to Left Pipe if he tries a back door feed.

Figure 6-35 – Ball Left Back – Correct Position: View from Left Back

During the following section, I'll talk about the ball coming from Right Back, and the same principles hold true for Left Back.

As the guy with the ball moves from X to Right Back, you have to move too. There are 3 main things you have to guard against:

1) Feeds out front,
2) Feeds to the back door, and
3) The ballhandler coming around the corner, beating his D-man and shooting.

Being in the right position to start with is key in defending against these possibilities. But each possibility then requires you to do different things and move to different spots.

1) Feeds to Out Front
Let's start with the simplest situation: The ballhandler has the ball at Right Back and feeds out front to either Right Top, Center Top or Left Top. The goalie – who of course is watching the ball intently, as I've discussed – turns counter-clockwise and sets up on the arc at the spot that's best for dealing with Ball Right Top, Center Top or Left Top.

Getting onto the right spot on the arc should take you as few steps and as little time as possible. See Figure 6-36 below:

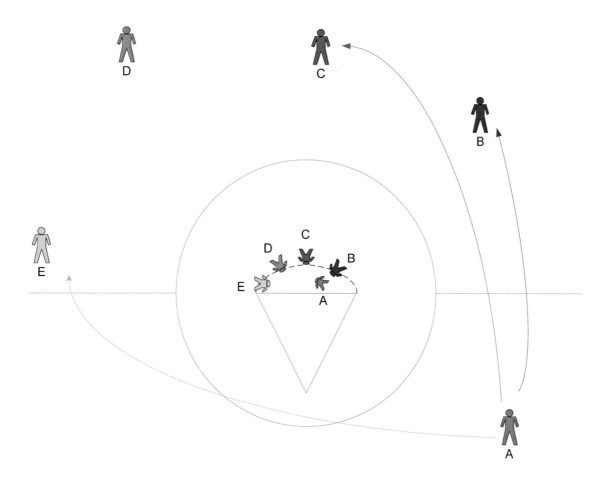

Figure 6-36 – Where to go for different feeds

Comments [If you don't have a color page, use the letters as reference]:

1) *When the ballhandler is at Right Back (A), the goalie stands where the red (A) goalie is.*
2) *When the "blue arrow" feed goes to the Blue Shooter (B), at Right Top, the Goalie goes to "Blue Goalie" (B) position.*
3) *For the Green feed to Center Top (C), he goes to Green Goalie (C).*
4) *For the Purple feed to Left Top (D), he goes to Purple Goalie (D).*
5) *For the Orange feed to the back side (E), he goes to Orange Goalie (E).*

It takes some practice to get to the right spot for every feed, but it's worth the time. The goalie needs to be set, in a good "ready to save" stance, on the correct spot on the arc, before the opponent catches the feed. As you move up to higher skill levels, attackers can catch a feed and fire a shot instantly, so you have to be ready. When a cutter is running fast at the goal and can quick-stick, he can easily shoot past you if you're late to the right spot.

2) Dealing with an Attacker coming at the corner, and the Back Door Feed

To guard against the feeds to the back side, if the ballhandler is coming from Right Back toward the Right Pipe area, you have to be careful not to move to the pipe too quickly. If you get too close to the right pipe, then you open up the back door too much. See Figure 6-37 below:

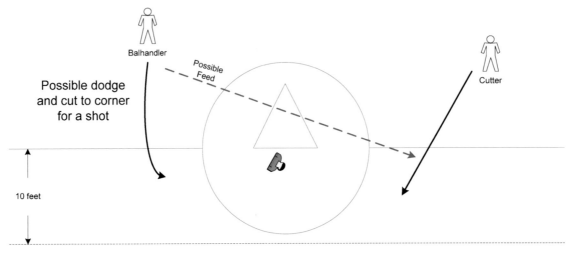

As ball moves to right back, face ball and get
closer to pipe to be ready for dodge and possible
shot as soon as guy clears corner,
BUT don't go all the way to the pipe til you have to,
because you have to guard against the feed to a
backside cutter

Figure 6-37 – Ball at Right Back

The photos below show what an open back door looks like and what happens if you leave it too open.

Figure 6-38 – Ball Right Back – Goalie needs to Watch the Backdoor

Comment: *Notice how open the back side is if you go to the pipe too soon when the ball is at Right Back.*

Figure 6-39 – End Result of a Backdoor Pass

Comment: *White Jersey on right pipe passed across to teammate on left pipe, who is taking left-handed shot. Goalie can't get from Right Pipe to Left Pipe fast enough.*

Here are some ways to deal with ball at Right Back:

When to move: I only move to the pipe when the ballhandler definitely looks like he wants to turn the corner and shoot. This takes some experience and judgment, but here are a couple of things to look for:

Ballhandler taking it slow: If the ballhandler is kind of gradually working his way from X to Right Back (or Left Back), seems to be looking to feed, and gets to about 3 feet behind GLE, I still don't jump to the pipe, as that would give away too much of the back side. It also helps to know if he's mainly a feeder or a dodger/shooter, and to determine how well your D-man is handling him. For example, if your D-man is overmatched, and the guy likes to drive to the corner, dodge and shoot, then you need to be ready for this. In this case, you'll also want to alert your defense to get ready to slide fast on the dodger. Finally, you might want to switch who's defending the guy – if you're lucky enough to have a better match-up.

Ballhandler charging at the corner: However, if he's charging from X or thereabouts toward Right Back and seems to be determined to come around the corner and shoot, OR if he's already beaten your D-man, then when he gets to 3 or 4 feet behind GLE (see Point A in Figure 6-40), I'll go right to the pipe, and get into "ready to save" stance fast.

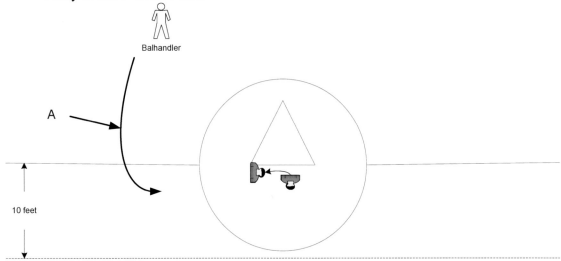

Figure 6-40 – When to get to the Pipe
Comment: Exactly when I go depends on the variables discussed in the text above and below: scouting report, e.g., Is he strictly a shooter?; How fast is he? Does he look like he's coming to shoot? Can my D-man turn him back? Etc.

Diagram: Figure 6-41 below shows another way to look at this is: Any time the ballhandler gets into the area in the shaded rectangle, the goalie needs to get to the pipe – but still watch out for the feed to the back side.

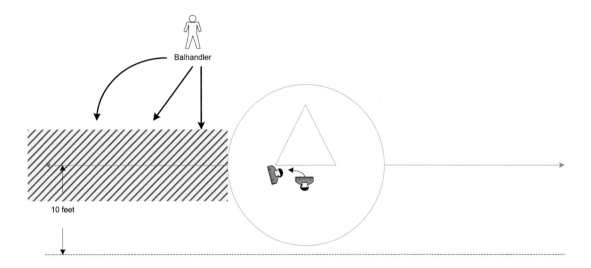

Balhandler

10 feet

Figure 6-41 – When to get to the Pipe (2)

BUT…Can he feed?: A guy who is dodging or about to dodge usually has his stick tucked in, protected – and he can't feed from there, so you don't have to worry about the backside as much as you have to worry about him coming around and shooting. See Figure 6-42 below:

Figure 6-42 – Ball Left Pipe – Goalie in Good Position
Comments: The ballhandler is clearly trying to dodge and is in no position to make a feed, so the goalie has made the right move – going to Left Pipe. If the ballhandler gets around his D-man, then the goalie is ready for a shot.

- <u>Feeder or Dodger?:</u> Most guys who handle the ball behind are either feeders or dodgers – and the goalie needs to treat each one differently. Either before the game in a scouting report, or early in the game, you have to figure out which type of threat each guy is. There are a few attackmen who are equally good at both. A couple years ago, I played in a Princeton Alumni vs. Varsity game. When Ryan Boyle got the ball at Right Back, I couldn't tell, *at all*, whether he was planning to feed or dodge and shoot – until the very last instant. All I knew was that he could do either one, so I was ready for both. The first time he had the ball, he came around, bulled past his D-man and shot – luckily I got a piece of it for the save. The next time, he looked exactly the same coming around the corner, but snapped a quick feed to a guy at Top Center. I managed to get in position fast for "ball at Top Front," and when the guy fired, I made the save.

  There are few guys as good as Ryan Boyle, but no matter what, anybody with the ball can score, regardless of whether you think a guy is better at feeding or dodging. After a guy comes around the corner and slams one by you because you were slow getting to the pipe, it doesn't do any good to say, "Hey the scouting report said that guy was mainly a feeder." In summary, it may help to know an opponent's tendencies, but you have to be ready for anything.

- <u>Come out or not?:</u> Another big-time controversy: When the ball is behind, and the attacker starts to turn the corner, one of the things goalies and coaches argue most about is "Do I come out on him, stay back, or something in between?" This situation is about the same as dealing with any one-on-one. There's no easy answer, and I'll talk about it some more in *Section 15.0 - One-on-Ones*, but here are a few things to think about for dealing with a shooter coming from behind:

  - <u>Watch the inside pipe:</u> The first rule of thumb is to always guard the inside pipe. If the shooter is coming from Right Back, I make sure my right foot is against the bottom of the pipe, and then go into my basic "ready to save" stance. I make sure there's no daylight between my right side and the pipe.

  - <u>Get to the pipe on time:</u> Once you see that the guy is driving hard to the corner, and probably wants to shoot, make your move. I recommend practicing this a lot. Just have a guy take the ball at X and drive right to the crease. Depending on how fast he's going, when he gets to 3-6 feet behind GLE, get to the pipe, fast, and get in position. The exact footwork for getting there may vary from goalie to goalie, but in general, you want to take as few steps as possible, and get into "ready to save" position immediately.

  - <u>Making the judgment:</u> Next, you'll have to make the crucial judgment call: Do I go out or stay back? In general, if you're playing against shooters with decent talent, it's a mistake to go out, unless they're right on top of you. Once you commit, they know where you are, and will just shoot at whatever part of the net isn't covered.

Figure 6-43 – Guarding the Pipe – When to go out

Comment: White Jersey attacker is rolling inside. Goalie needs to decide whether to go out and nail him or guard the pipe. This goalie appears to have given up on the pipe and is about to go out.

<u>Is the shooter ready to fire?:</u> The other thing to look for is: "Is the shooter cocked and ready to shoot?" If he's just finished a tough dodge and just bulled past your D-man, or pulled the "inside roll" move, and if his stick isn't yet in a position he can shoot from, AND if he's close enough for you to reach him, then by all means, take a fast step or two out, and lay into him before he can lock and load.

<u>If you go, go hard:</u> When you decide to do this, go hard. Don't just wave your stickhead at him or his stick: Go out straight and sharp with your stick, lower your shoulder, and go for the middle of his body. I don't mean for you to try to hurt him – there's no place for cheap shots in lacrosse – but hey, it's a contact sport, and if a guy gets too close to your crease, it's often a good idea to give him a nice clean hit.

See Figure 6-44 (*When to Go Out on a Guy Coming at the Corner* - below). If the attacker gets near or in the shaded circle and doesn't look like he's going to feed, then go for him. Note that it's a fairly small circle – maybe 3 or 4 feet in diameter in this drawing. The size will vary depending on how fast you are, how fast he's running, how ready he is to shoot, how good he is, etc.

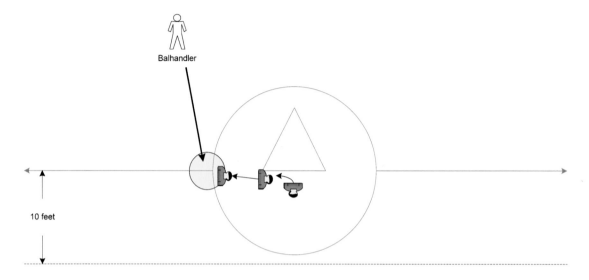

Balhandler

10 feet

Figure 6-44 – When to Go Out on a Guy Coming at the Corner

I recommend practicing this – Have guys come around the corner and learn how to step out and nail them. It doesn't have to be a bloodbath, but you need to try it a lot during practice. It's good for you and your attackmen.

- When to stay back: BUT, if the shooter dodged the D-man somewhere back near X and has had time to get his stick ready to shoot, and isn't coming within 3 or so feet of the crease as he comes around, then I recommend holding your ground, guarding the inside pipe, and getting in your best "ready to save" stance. Hopefully, a slide will come in a second, but if it doesn't, all you can do is improve your odds. Here are a couple things to try in this situation:

- Watching his stick position: When a guy comes around the corner unguarded, his stick will be in one of three general areas: high, hip-height or low.

    1) Stickhead High: If his stickhead is high, I keep in my normal stance but make sure that my stickhead stays high.
        a. *High shot:* If he shoots high, at least I have a chance at it. If he shoots low, then I might not have time to get the stickhead down, but I rely on my feet and legs – more on the feet in *Section 7.0 – Stepping to the Ball, and Section 20.1 - My Unorthodox Technique on Low Shots.*

b. *Low Shot:* See Figure 6-45 below: This picture shows a shot where I can't get my stick down in time, but have "snapped" my legs together to make the low save with my foot, shin, knee or thigh.

Figure 6-45 – Feet together on the low save move

Comment: This move has bailed me out again and again. The fact is that some shots are just too fast to get a stick on. But, by constant practice, I eventually got to the point where I could often snap my legs together quickly enough to make the save.

c. *Waist Level Shot:* If the shot comes at me at waist level, I might not be able to get my stick down in time, and my feet and shins won't do any good, but I've often been able to use my legs to drive my thigh or one side of my midsection into the path of the shot.

2) Stickhead Hip-High: Guys sometimes come around the corner with the stickhead at hip height. In this case, I use pretty much the same approach as when his stickhead is high: I keep my stickhead high for the high shots, feet and legs ready for a low ball, and midsection or thigh for in between.

3) Stickhead Low: One thing I've seen a lot is guys breaking free from a D-man, speeding to the corner with their knees bent, and trying to whip in a low sidearm shot. (Sometimes they even dive and shoot as they get near the ground.) This is the one case where I'll drop my stick down and "get big" down low. If the distance between his stickhead and me is only a few feet, then getting my big crosse in the way cuts down the angle with a lot more surface area than my legs. I stay in the "ready to save" stance, but have my stickhead right down next to my left calf (remember, I'm left-handed). Even if he's able to get off a shot that's heading high, my cutting off the angle often snuffs this shot before it goes too far. And, as always, if I miss the low shot with my stick, I'm ready to snap my legs together to make a foot or leg save.

- Another reason to stick to the pipe: If a right-handed shooter is peeling hard to the crease from Right Back, and moving from the goalie's right to left, his shot will often have a tendency to go to the goalie's left. So if you don't give him the near pipe, and he has to shoot for the far pipe, the ball has a better chance of going wide. (The best players can shoot anywhere from anywhere, but I'm talking here about general tendencies of most players.)

When you see the shot coming, you know it will come one of three places:

- To your right – you know this shot will miss because you have the pipe covered. You still go for the shot, of course, but it'll be wide if you're on the pipe.
- Right at you, which are fine – just make a save move, catch the shot, or get hit to make the body save.
- To your left – in this case, you obviously have to make the save move for the offside (if you're right-handed) shot.

In summary, sticking to the pipe means you're cutting off one of the shooter's options, and you can make the save by either standing still or going offside.

6.3 After a Missed Shot

A goalie's position is important not only before the shot, but also afterwards, for example:

1) On the wide or high shot that misses the goal and zips past untouched.

2) On an uncontrolled save, e.g., a rebound off a bounce shot, or a shot that goes high in the air after you get a piece of your stick on it.

Let's take a look at each of these situations.

6.3.1 Wide and High Shots

There I am in my "ready to save" stance, the shooter fires one, and it goes wide or high of the goal. My first move is to whip my head around to see where the ball is heading. One of several things can happen:

1) Opponent gets it right away: If an opponent who's backing up the goal catches the errant shot at, say, Right Back, then I get right into the position I should be in for any time a ballhandler has the ball at Right Back (see Figure 6-46 below). I also yell to my defense some code word that tells them that the attack has the ball

again and we need to get right back into our defensive set-up. A lot of D-men and long-stick middies tend to relax for a second when they see a shot go wide – but it only takes a second for their man to get open, take a quick feed from the guy backing up the goal, and shoot.

Figure 6-46 – Goalie watches shot that went wide

Comment: Goalie will stay in crease and not chase the loose ball because the attacker should easily get to it first.

2) <u>When to go for the loose ball:</u> If the errant shot isn't going that fast, I have to decide whether or not to chase it. If I can get to the loose ball before anybody else, and have enough time to get a clear started before getting hit, then I'll go for the ball. Note that if the goalie leaves the crease to chase a ground ball, a D-man needs to stay in the Hole – see Figure 6-47 below.

Figure 6-47 – When Goalie chases a shot, a D-man needs to stay in the Hole

But if there's an attackman and a D-man right near the ball, then I'll usually hang back and stay in position, because if I run out of the crease and get involved in a fight for the ground ball, and if the attacker gets it, then that leaves the goal open, with no goalie in sight. One quick feed out front and they score. Plus my D-man has a 50-50 chance of getting it anyway. See Figure 6-48 below:

Figure 6-48 – Loose Ball: Goalie stays in crease because he has three D-men who have a good shot at getting the ball.

3) <u>Chasing the shot that goes Out of Bounds (OB)</u>: If the wide or high shot is really screaming, and if I see that nobody is going to catch it, then I normally turn the corner and run as fast as I can directly to where the ball is going to go OB. You'd think that there'd always be an attackman backing up shots, but that's not the case, even at high levels of lacrosse. Over the years, I've just about always ended up running down shots OB at least a few times a game. We get the ball and have a chance to clear, which beats worrying about shooters.

Figure 6-49 – Shot Wide –
Goalie has been watching the shot go wide and takes off

Figure 6-50 – Shot Wide – When you go, go hard

4) <u>Know the field conditions:</u> There are a couple of field-specific things that you need to think about before the game, which might affect whether or not you chase these shots.

   a. <u>Slow field:</u> First, on a "soft" field or one with long grass, be careful before you chase a wide shot into the back corner or the sidelines. You think that the shot is definitely going OB, you take off and run 20 yards or so, but the ball gets hung up in the grass, and you end up in no man's land, chasing a ground ball, and getting whacked by a couple attackmen. One of them gets the loose ball and feeds back out front, long before you can get back to the goal.

   b. <u>Fast field:</u> Second, on a dry hard field or on artificial turf, the opposite is true: A shot that would stay in bounds on a normal field will keep running – so you can chase these hard, rather than hanging back.

6.3.2 The Uncontrolled Save - Rebounds

A middie winds up and fires from out front. You make a great move and get a piece of it with your stick, elbow, glove, facemask or whatever - and the ball goes….somewhere. Now what?

With experience, a goalie learns to "feel" where a rebound is going. You can't learn this in a book, but only by taking a lot of warm-up and playing for hours on end. As you learn and practice more to develop that experience, here are a couple things to think about:

1) <u>Is it out front?:</u> The most dangerous place for a rebound to go is out in front of the goal. So if you have no clue at all where the ball went, always look out front first – and get into your "ready to save" stance right away.

2) <u>Figuring it out:</u> Given the height and type of shot, and the move you just made to get a piece of it, you can make a good guess about where the rebound went. For example, if it's an offside low shot, and you get your stick over just in time to have the shot hit the shaft, if you've slanted your shaft "downward" (see Figure 5-22 above), then you can predict that the ball should bounce out low.

   On the other hand, if the shot was offside hip, and you made that move to your left (if you're right-handed), then usually you'll be bringing your stick sideways and possibly upwards as you catch a piece of the ball – which means the rebound will often go to the left and/or up in the air. But this doesn't always happen, because balls can really bounce anywhere. I've had saves where I was moving my stick to left, but the ball hit the wall and bounced out to the right.

   I don't know a perfect way to predict rebounds – experience helps, and watching the ball into the mesh will at least have you looking at the right place.

Figure 6-51 – Knowing Where the Rebound Went

3) <u>Planning ahead:</u> Before the game, you can talk with your defense (including middies) and make sure they call the ball location out to you on rebounds, if it looks to them like you don't know where the rebound went. The only negative to this is that the offense might not know where it is either, so the D should yell the location only if they think that you have a good chance of getting to it before anybody else (e.g., when a rebound goes almost straight up, over top of your head). Otherwise, if the attackers look as confused as the goalie, the D-men should say nothing and go after the ball themselves.

Before the game, you and the D can agree on a code word, like "Red," to indicate that the ball is in the most dangerous part of the field – right in front of the goal. The first defenseman to see the ball there yells out "Red" so that everybody (except the opponent) knows where to look.

(Off subject a little, but worth mentioning: A corollary to this is if a ballhandler drops the ball and doesn't know it. The tendency is to immediately yell out "Ball down," but it's better to wait a second or two, and give the *former* ballhandler time to continue to run away from the ball (thinking he still has it). By this time, your D-man will see the ground ball and/or you can then yell "Ball down," and the D-man won't have to fight the former ballhandler for it. A long time ago, I stopped immediately telling attackmen they'd dropped the ball, and it's gotten my teams a lot of extra possessions.)

91

6.4 Ball Downfield

When my attack has the ball downfield in our offensive end, I go out to the top of the crease or even farther out, rather than hanging back in a flat or medium arc. This positions me a few feet closer to any ball that suddenly flies down into our defensive end.

Some goalies go pretty far outside the crease (10 or 20 feet), to get even closer to a possible long pass or loose ball. This is fine, as long as you can get back into position when the opponents' attackers get control and start working the ball around. If you come too far out of the crease, the opponent will try to work an attacker in behind you. If he catches a quick feed and beats his D-man, then you'll probably have too far to come back to get in position to make the save.

In either case, when our offense has the ball, the goalie still has to keep an eye on the opponent's attackmen. A D-man will often fall asleep and let his man drop several yards behind him, which puts the attackman in position to take a quick pass and run in on the goalie one-on-one. So…if you see an attacker sneaking away from his man, yell at your D-man to get back on him.

7.0 Stepping to the Ball

OK, let's recap again: You've got that great positive attitude going, got decent gear on, and you know where to position yourself when the ball's out front or behind.

Making a save consists of doing several things right – focusing, watching the ball, being in the right stance, stepping to the ball, moving your stick to the right place at the right time, and then finishing the save by controlling the ball. That sounds like a lot of moving parts, but as you practice, you'll find that all the different pieces fit together and start to flow into a single coordinated save move.

One thing to keep in mind as you read about the different aspects of making a save: Each part of the save move needs to be compact and efficient, so that the entire move becomes as quick and sharp as possible. When making a save, there's no time for wasted motion – no hopping when you step, no "looping" as you drive the stickhead to the ball, no "rocking back before you step, no "hitches" in the move. So let's begin with the first step to the ball – keep it sharp, quick, compact – just like the rest of the save move will be.

7.1   Step to the Ball - Basics

For those of you who are just starting: Stepping to the ball is really important if you want to become a decent goalie. For those of you who have played a while: You probably heard that message a million times, but it's still just as important.

In principle, it's simple: When you see the shot coming, step out into the line of the shot with the foot closest to the ball. This goes for all shots – high, hip-high, low, and everywhere in between. Stepping gets the rest of your body moving to be in position to make the save. And if you can't get your stick to the shot in time, stepping into the shot line lets you make the save with your foot, leg or some other body part.

Also, from harsh experience, I can tell you that stepping to the ball tightens the quad (on the front of the thigh), so that if the ball hits you there, it hurts a lot less than if your quad is relaxed – which is what happens if you don't step. Try a quick experiment: Stand relaxed and push on your quad – it will be soft and unflexed. Then step forward, bending your knee forward and putting weight on your foot – the quad flexes and is much harder.

Figures 7-1 and 7-2 show the general idea of "stepping to the ball."

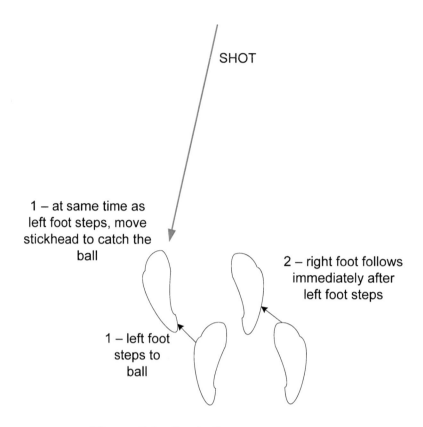

SHOT

1 – at same time as left foot steps, move stickhead to catch the ball

2 – right foot follows immediately after left foot steps

1 – left foot steps to ball

Figure 7-1 – Basic Stepping to the Ball

Figure 7-2 – Stepping to the Ball:

First step is with left foot as he snaps the stick down. "Back" (right) foot will then step next to stickhead.

Figure 7-3 – Stepping to the ball

Attacker on far right has just shot. Ball is in center of photo (in black circle). Goalie has stepped to the shot and is bringing his stick down at the same time as he's stepping.

In practice, of course, there are some finer points to talk about.

Don't Hop: First, one common mistake I see is goalies who kind of "hop" when they step. They pick their feet up higher than they have to when taking the first and/or the second step. This wastes time and can allow a shot to go under your foot before you finish the step. Instead of "hopping," I step low and straight, barely lifting my cleats above the ground. Before the shot, my knees are bent in my "ready to save" stance, and they stay bent as I step to the ball. (The one exception is on a high shot where I might have to straighten my leg to reach up and over to the ball.)

"Attack the Ball": Second, note that you step out toward the ball, not sideways. Stepping out to the ball cuts down the angle, and gets your body in a better position to stop the shot in case you miss with your stick. Also, on bounce shots, it gets your stickhead out to the ball sooner, before it can take a bad hop. This is very similar to infielders who don't "let the ball play them" (i.e., back off from a grounder), get set and then make the play. See Figure 7-5 below for how NOT to step:

Figure 7-4 – Step <u>out toward the ball</u>….
NOT sideways….see Figure 7-5 below: though there is a possible exception…

SHOT

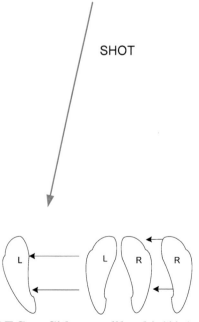

Figure 7-5 – DO NOT Step Sideways like this!!! (<u>unless</u>…see text below)

The only time I step sideways: For you more advanced goalies, there may be an exception to this. For example, if a shooter gets off a real rocket that's heading offside low, right toward that farthest, lowest corner of the goal, and if I judge that stepping <u>out</u> to the ball will get my foot and/or my stick there too late to stop it, then I confess that I'll step sideways to intercept the shot just before it goes in.

Figure 7-6 - Not much of a step…but I made the save

Comments: This shot was really ripped from close in, and, as you can see, I didn't have time to step out to the ball with my left foot. BUT at least I did push off my right foot toward my left, which helped me get my stick-wall in the way for the save. Not a really pretty sight, and not as good as controlling the save, but beats getting scored on.

People sometimes give me a hard time for this - "Hey – you stepped sideways!" - but it's better than having to turn around and rake the ball out of the goal. I've used this move to make a fair number of foot saves in the low corners. Maybe my stick is just too slow to get there. In any case, it works for me, and you can try it if you're finding that you're having a hard time making these low corner saves. It also helps that I've practiced that move many thousands of times. So until you've done that or unless you've already had some success with going sideways, 99% of the time, you should always step OUT toward the ball.

Stepping brings the body into play: I always try to step right in line with the shot – that way, if I can't get my stick to the ball in time, then my foot, leg, midsection, head or some other body part will at least be lined up to stop the shot. With new goalies, and especially on higher shots that look easy to just catch, there's often a tendency to not step, and just reach out with the stick to make the catch.

The problem with this is that if you don't make that "easy catch," and the ball comes off the edge of your stickhead, then it will often bounce right into the goal – and since you didn't step, your body isn't there to stop the rebound. But if you step to the ball, this will always bring your body into the general line of the shot and you'll stop a lot more shots that miss, or glance off, the stickhead.

Figure 7-7 – Stepping brings the body into the shot line

Comment: When my left foot steps up to the side of the stickhead, I've maximized the amount of surface area that can stop the shot. My right foot has stepped right in line with the shot, and I've snapped my stick down to also be in the shotline. Some goalies and coaches would advise me to snap the stickhead down about 3" farther to my left, but I have unorthodox reasons for my approach, which I'll discuss in Section 20.1.
In any case, the main point is that by stepping to the ball with my lead foot, and bringing my back foot up, I bring as much of my body as possible in the way of the shot.

7.2   Low Shots

So if you step out with your right foot, what do you do with your "back" (in this case, your left) foot (and vice versa, of course)? On low shots, most coaches and goalies will recommend bringing your stickhead down next to your right foot, and bring the left foot beside the left side of the net – so that your stickhead is between your legs (see Figure 7-8 below).

Figure 7-8 – One foot on each side of stickhead.
Get the top edge of the stickhead all the way to the ground

Make sure you drive your stickhead right to the ground so the ball can't skip underneath it. (This low skipping happens a lot on wet grass and on low sidearm shots.) If your stickhead is down onto the ground, then on a bounce shot, the ball will normally bounce right into your mesh so you can make the save. See Figure 7-9 below.

Figure 7-9 –Top edge of the stickhead all the way down

But if the ball takes a higher-than-expected bounce above the stickhead/mesh, then you just bring the stickhead up, using your arms and/or your legs. If your stick is already all the way down to the ground, it's a lot easier to get these high bouncers than it is to have your stickhead, say, 6 inches above the ground, and then try to go down to stop a shot that's going under it. <u>Snatching down at the ball is seldom successful.</u>

7.2.1 Standard Stepping Technique on Low Shots

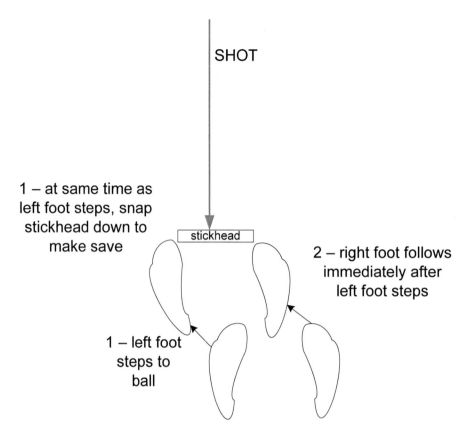

Figure 7-10 – Stepping to Save the Low Shot

Figure 7-11 – Stepping to the offside
low shot

Figure 7-12 – Stepping to the stick-side
low shot

Comments: Note that the first step is out to the ball, and the stickhead is snapped down at the same time. Back foot will then step up to the other side of the stickhead.

7.2.2 Low Shots – Controlling Rebounds

Whichever technique you prefer, a couple other things hold true.

On low and bounce shots, when you step, keep your knees bent, and keep your upper body leaning forward - without losing your balance, of course (see Figure 7-13 and 7-14 below). On low shots, angle your stick so that a rebound off the stick will drop right in front of you. This will happen more naturally if in your "ready to save" stance, you've been holding your lower hand farther out from your body than your upper hand (as mentioned in Section 5.2.5).

Figure 7-13 – Angling the stick so that rebounds will drop right in front of you: Moderate Angle

Figure 7-14 – Angling the stick so that rebounds will drop right in front of you: Severe Angle, favored by some goalies, should make the ball rebound almost straight down, right under the mesh.

If the butt-end of your stick is angled back toward to goal, then a rebound will have a much better chance of either bouncing off the stick and right into the goal, or going up and out back toward all those shooters waiting around the crease. You have a much better chance of controlling a rebound if you're in the following position: Knees bent, butt end of stick angled forward, upper body leaning forward or "bent over" a bit.

7.3 Hip-high Shots

The footwork on onside and offside hip-high shots is basically the same as for low shots: You step to the ball and bring your back foot up. On hip-high shots, my technique is to bring the feet together, but many people prefer and recommend that the back foot end up about 12 – 16 inches from the lead foot. This helps to maintain balance. (In case you're wondering, with my feet together I keep my balance largely by conditioning my legs and from having practiced this stepping thousands of times.)

7.4 High Shots

Same deal here: Step to the ball and bring up the back foot. You may have noticed that there's a theme running through all this talk about footwork: ALWAYS step out to the ball, and always bring that back foot up.

Summary:
Section 7.0 may seem like a lot of time spent talking about stepping, but it's that important. Next we'll start to make the rest of the "save move" and finish the save.

8.0 Goalie Stickwork

8.1 Making the Save

OK, now you've stepped to the ball, and here it comes. I won't kid you – it's not all that easy to make a clean save of a 90 mph shot. The main key to getting good at this is to practice.

8.1.1 Basics

First, though, let's make sure you cover the basics:

1) As mentioned in *Section 2.0 – Equipment*, you need a decent stick. It doesn't have to be the most expensive, and by the way, the fanciest stick in the store won't make you any better if you don't practice. To repeat what I said earlier: You want a fairly deep pocket, but not so deep that you can't pass with it.

2) You have to focus on what's going on.

3) You have to watch the ball.

4) You have to be in a good stance, and in the right position on the arc – and then step out to the ball.

How many times do I need to say all that? Well, until you're doing it all the time, without having to think about it. I still remind myself of these basics before every game.

Here are a few ideas that can improve your ability to make clean saves:

- Watch the ball, all the time: If you're new or fairly new to the game, you have to learn to catch the ball before you learn to control saves. When you're just playing catch, try watching the ball all the way into the net. If your eyes are following the ball all the way, it tends to almost magically put the stick in the right place to make the save. Then try the same thing when you're warming up: You're already watching the ball (right?), so focus on watching it all the way.

- "Practice" off the practice field: Play catch with other people as much as you can.

- Wall ball: Play wall ball a lot. Even when nobody else is around, you can work on saves from every angle – high, low; right, left; fast, faster.

- Get used to it: Note that I recommend you play in all your gear as often as possible. OK, sure, if you're just tossing the ball around in the yard, you don't need a chest protector, but especially for new guys, the more you wear gloves, helmet, etc., the faster you'll get used to it.

- <u>Soft hands:</u> Make sure you don't bat out at the ball – you're not playing tennis or baseball. Earlier I talked about having your hands and arms at least a little ways out from the body: This allows you to get the stickhead into the ball's path, and then "give" a little with your arms and hands just as the ball hits the mesh, and instantly go into the cradle, which will control the ball.
In summary, the whole body is involved in making a controlled save. The trick is to practice a lot until you don't leave out any of the aspects of the save and until this is completely natural.

- <u>Goalies live between the pipes:</u> Finally, warm up a lot in the cage. I'll talk about practice and pre-game warm-ups more in Sections 18.1 and 19.0, but as far as controlling saves goes, early in your career, the best thing you can do is see a lot of shots coming at you. But….see below:

- ***Coaches need to read this too*** - <u>Watch out for TOO much:</u> Goalies can get <u>gun-shy or shell-shocked</u>. This happens, especially to newer goalies, if they spend way too much time getting shot at, getting hit and hurt, and eventually feeling sore and humiliated.
The first symptoms of being gun-shy are not stepping to the ball, stepping so that the body isn't in line with the shot, and/or ducking the head out of the way.
If this starts to happen to you, then you need to take a break from the goal. Tell your coach that you need to back off for a half hour or so, or even for a whole practice.
To get over being gun-shy, here's what I recommend:
    1) Have a nice, relaxing catch with a teammate for 10 or 15 minutes.

    2) During this catch, go back to focusing on the fundamentals: Watch the ball, step to the ball, watch the ball into the mesh.

    3) Go back to the nets, get into your ready-to-save stance. Remind yourself to watch the ball and step to the shot.

    4) Have your coach or teammate give you an easy warm-up – no hard shots. During the warm-up, focus on being in your stance, watching the ball, stepping to the shot, and watching the ball into the mesh.

    5) Don't rush through this warm-up. After each shot, take a deep breath, relax, toss the ball back to the shooter, and take your time in getting back into the right stance and getting ready for the next shot.

    6) Don't take any hard shots for a day if you don't feel up to it.

This routine should help you get over being gun-shy. Other people may have some other ideas, but this is what worked for me early in my career. If you're new and have had some bouts with being gun-shy, I can only tell you to hang in there, go back to the basics, and work through it – if you really want to be a goalie. As goalies get more experience, being gun-shy usually disappears. If it never goes away, then it's possible that you're not cut out to be a goalie. Don't feel bad: Most people aren't. But you can still enjoy lacrosse at another position, so there's no need to quit the sport just because you have sense enough to not want to get hit with shots.

Now let's look at each of the main types of save a goalie will be making.

8.1.2 Low and Bounce Shots

8.1.2.1   Stick-side Low

It seems that any stick-side shot would be easier to save than an offside shot. But this isn't always the case. The main mistakes I've seen goalies make on the stick-side low shot – and how to work on avoiding or correcting these errors - are:

1) Not stepping to the ball: Maybe we goalies have a tendency to think, "Oh this shot is stick-side, so I'll just get my stick over to it – no need to step." This is a bad habit to get into. The only way around it is to always step to the ball, even when the save looks "easy."

2) "Waving" or "snatching" at the ball: I see this a lot, especially on stick-side bounce shots. The goalie seems to think that he can snatch that bounce shot in midair, makes a stab at it, and misses. A goalie who does this snatching is usually standing up too straight as well. Again, this is a really bad habit to get into – in fact, it's often two bad habits: snatching and standing up straight.
Here are three main causes of and solutions to this problem:

   a) Knees bent: Focus on keeping your stick-side knee bent when you step to the stick-side shot. This will keep your body low, and prevent you from straightening up too much.

   b) Arms out: If your hands, arms and elbows are tucked in close to your body, you'll tend to have harder time getting your stickhead all the way down.

   c) Stick low: Concentrate on keeping your stickhead low: By this I mean that when you snap your stick down to make the save, the top edge of stickhead should be hit, and be parallel to, the ground. I make sure mine actually touches the ground. If the ball skips low, then your stickhead is already down, and you can make the save.

If the ball bounces up, then you can raise your stickhead a) with your arms, and b) by straightening your knees a bit as the ball comes closer. It's a lot easier to handle a bounce or low shot by coming from a low stickhead, than by having your stickhead too high (say, 6 to 12 inches above the ground) and trying to snatch down at it.

Figure 8-1 – Basic Stick-side Low save move:
First step with right foot, snap stickhead to the ground. Tom's left foot will follow and end up next to stickhead.

Figure 8-2 – Basic Stick-side Low save move:
I first step with left foot (since I'm left-handed), as I snap my stickhead to the ground. My right foot will follow by stepping up next to the stickhead.

3) <u>Not practicing stick-side enough:</u> Goalies and coaches tend to think that the stick-side save is easy, so they don't spend much time on it. As you'll see in Sections 18.1 and 19.0, warm-ups need to cover this shot just as much as any other.

8.1.2.2   *Off-side Low*

The off-side low shot can be tough, especially when you face a shooter who can hit the far bottom corner of the cage. This is a move I've practiced probably more than any other, because:

1) In college and a lot of club ball, shooters can definitely hit the offside low corner, and
2) A goalie has to do everything right to catch up with the shot.

<u>To break this save move down</u>…first let's assume that you're in a great, balanced stance, ready to go either way, your eyes are lasered in on the ball, you're focused on what's going on, your arms, hands, and elbows are in the right place, you've been doing all your

108

conditioning, you've practiced this move (along with all the others) until you can barely stand up – and all those other things we've talked about:

1a) <u>First Step:</u> It all starts with the first step. I try to get my first step right into the path of the shot. In my "ready to save" stance, my stick-head is right up next to my helmet, so has a long way to go to reach the off-side low area. My foot has a lot less distance to travel, so I can often at least get a toe in the way, even if my stick is late.

1b) <u>Snap Stick Down:</u> As I'm making that first step, I snap my stick down to the offside with everything I've got. This brings up the point that, when moving the stick to make a save, I do it in one fast move.

2) <u>Stick to the Ground:</u> As with the stick-side low shot, the stickhead stays low throughout the move, so that when it gets to the ball, the top edge of the wall is against the ground.

Figure 8-3 – Basic Offside Low save move:
First step with left foot, snap stickhead to the ground. Right foot will follow and end up next to stickhead. Note that Tom's head is still down, watching the ball.

3) <u>Back Foot:</u> The instant that my first step is made and planted, I follow with my back foot. This provides extra momentum and therefore speed to the overall move. On occasion, I've also made the save with the back foot – I nick the shot with my stickhead, and the ball slows down just a little, which gives my back foot time to kick it away as I'm taking that second step. As noted above in Section 7.1, when making this move, it's especially important not to "hop" when you step, but to keep the feet close to the ground. If you hop, you'll be late to the ball, you might step

right over the ball instead of in its path, and overall you have a lot worse chance of making the foot save.

4)   Eyes still on the ball: Watch the ball into the mesh.

5)   "Finishing" the Save: By "finishing" I mean catching the ball, controlling the save, and coming up ready to look for the outlet pass. On low shots, you have two choices:

   a. *Go for the clean, controlled save:* The best choice, of course, is to catch the ball cleanly. I don't know of any special magic trick to teach on this – it just takes lots of hours of practice. Wall ball is great for this: I hate to tell you how many hours of wall ball I played, throwing the ball so that low, hard shots were flying back at me – stick-side, off-side, 5-hole.
   The only bit of technique that might be worth mentioning is that as soon as the ball hits my mesh, I need to go right into a controlled cradle. This involves dropping the bottom hand (the one near the butt end of the stick) down, which keeps the ball from bouncing out of the mesh. As this hand drops down, I curl the wrist of the top hand in as I start to cradle. By the way, I still don't control all those low shots, but I'm getting better…

   b. *Play for the controlled rebound:* If you can't make the controlled save, or you have trouble catching low shots, then angle your stickhead toward the ground (as mentioned above), don't worry about trying to catch the ball, just let the ball hit the mesh and bounce down right in front of you. Scoop or rake the ball up, and then go into your clear. This isn't as good as a fully controlled save, but it's certainly better than missing the ball entirely; letting the ball rebound straight out 5 feet in front of the crease; or trying to catch it, losing control and watching the ball fly off who-knows-where.

Whether you go for the clean save or the controlled rebound will depend on the following:

   1) How good you are at making a clean catch of the low shot. The more you practice, the better you'll get.

   2) How quickly you can get the stick to the right position for the clean save. Sometimes, no matter how good you usually are at the low save, a great shot will make it impossible to make a clean catch. In this case, I just go for angling my stick down and trying to control the rebound.

8.1.2.3   5-Hole Low
The save move on the shot to the 5-hole is similar to the move to offside low – you just don't have to go as far with your step or your stickhead. One thing to make sure you

practice though is: If a shot is coming straight at my 5-hole, which foot do I step with first?

In theory, it doesn't matter – the answer is: whichever foot will lead you to make the best, fastest move. To find this out, I've tried it both ways, and settled on what works best for me (off-side foot – just as if I'm going for an off-side low shot). But this may be different for you, so try both, see what feels right, ask people to tell you which way looks faster, decide, and practice a lot.

Figure 8-4 – Basic 5-Hole save move:
The first step and snap-down of the stickhead. Left foot will follow, next to stickhead.

Figure 8-5 – Basic 5-Hole save move: The second step.

Comment: *One <u>negative</u> in this photo is that my left foot is 3 or 4 inches too far forward. I'm leaving this "incorrect" photo here to make a point: Don't step out too far past your stickhead because if you have to raise the stickhead up on a bounce shot, the inside part of your legs can get in the way. Other than that, the position in the picture is covering the 5-hole pretty well, so read on…:*

Notice how little empty space is left between my legs for the ball to get through.

1) *If ball takes a higher-than-expected bounce, I can block any empty space by raising the stickhead with (a) a quick straightening of my legs and/or (b) a fast lift with my hands and arms.*

2) *If ball unexpectedly kicks to my right, then my right arm and elbow are in position to make a quick "flick" and block the shot. Note that this works a lot better with my elbow "out" – as in the photo above – than if my elbow is tucked in really close to my body. This is yet another good reason for keeping the elbows and arms out from the body when in the initial ready-to-save stance: If I make the right save move, then my elbow ends up as you see it in the picture above: Note how my right arm and elbow are blocking out more of the net than if my elbow were close to my side. Even if I don't move my arm and elbow with the "flick" I mentioned, they could still get in the way of a bad bounce and make the save.*

3) *If ball takes a bad hop to my left, then I can "wing out" my left arm to stop it.*

These 3 moves take a lot of practice, but become second-nature after a few hundred or thousand reps.

8.1.3 Bounce Shots

The moves to Stick-side, Off-side, and 5-Hole bounce shots are similar to what I do to save low shots. But here are a couple notes about what makes bounce shots different:

- Hard or soft ground: Check out how the ball is bouncing during pre-game warm-up because field conditions affect bounce shots.

  - Wet grass will sometimes cause the ball to "skip low" instead of bouncing as high as it would on normal ground. This gives the goalie all the more reason to keep the top edge of stickhead right down to the ground when making the low save.

  - On the other hand, if your region has been in a dry spell, the ground might be extremely hard, which will cause the ball to bounce higher than usual. You still want to keep your stickhead down on low shots, but just be ready for the high bounce.

- Grounds-keeping in the crease: Pay close attention to what the ground in front of the goal looks like. If it's nice and smooth or if you're playing on turf, then that's great – most bounce shots will hit the ground and go straight. But if there are lump from dried mud, clods of dirt, stones, etc., I always clean the mess out from in front of the goal and try to smooth down the bumpier areas. Even the smallest pea-sized pebble can cause a bad hop that goes in the goal.

- Shooter's release angle: If an attackman shoots straight overhand, then usually the ball will bounce high. If he comes underhand or sidearm, then the bounce will be at a lower angle. Either way, I still use the same stance and save moves – but watching the shooter's wind-up will allow me to anticipate what's coming.

8.1.4 Hip-High (or "Hip") Shots

For hip-high (or just "hip") shots, I use about the same stepping and moves as I do for low shots. The main difference, of course, is that instead of making sure my stickhead is down to the ground, I just have to catch the ball. Here are a few comments about handling the different hip shots.

8.1.4.1   Stick-side Hip-High

This should be the easiest save in the book. Goalies miss these usually just because they aren't watching the ball closely enough.

Another thing I see happen sometimes is that the goalie gets the plastic of his stickhead on the ball, but the plastic bends a little. The ball glances off the wall and goes in. To avoid this, make sure your stickhead wall is firm and stiff. Note that hot weather will make it softer and more pliable, so test it out in 90 degrees if you play in a hot area. A head might be fine in March, when it's 50 out, but turn into Silly Putty in May.

Sometimes the goalie makes a good move but lets the stickhead get knocked back by a hard shot. Again, the ball rebounds into the goal. It's great to have soft hands, but that doesn't mean holding the stick so loosely that it can get banged out of position. Like just about everything else, practice will cure this: You'll find the line between "giving" too much with the stick and holding it firmly enough to avoid this problem.

Figure 8-6 – Basic Stick-side Hip save move

Figure 8-7 – Finishing the Stick-side Hip save move –
Watching the ball into the mesh. Note also that as soon as the ball has hit the mesh,
Tom is going into a cradle move to control the ball.

114

8.1.4.2   Off-side Hip-High
This can be a tough save if you aren't in a good stance, don't step, and especially if your arms, hands and/or elbows are too close to your body. This move takes a lot of practice, just like off-side low.

Figure 8-8 – Offside Hip, waist-level – good move, for a glove save.
(Ball is just to our right of the pipe, after hitting glove.)

Figure 8-9 – Offside Hip, just below waist – Nice Save.
Stepped to ball, Knees bent, Watched ball into mesh. Lowering left hand as he goes into the cradle to control the save.

Figure 8-10 – Offside Hip, Above waist

Comment: Note that this shot came in between hip and shoulder height. The goalie can go with the "across the face" save move for offside high shots, or – as I did in this case - with the same move you'd want to use for offside hip-high. Either way, a couple of principles stay the same: step to the ball and watch it into the stick.

8.1.4.3   Straight-at-you, Hip-High

This one should be fairly easy too. But sometimes, I see a goalie actually step away from this shot to make it easier to get his stickhead in the center, on the ball. The ball hits the edge of the wall and bounces in because the goalie's body isn't behind the stickhead, in line with the shot. This may happen largely because this is what's natural to do when we're playing catch. But being a goalie is different, and sometimes you have to do what seems unnatural – and then practice the right move until it overcomes your initial bad tendency. The moral of the story is to always step out toward the ball, never away from it. This will keep your body in line with the shot so you'll make a body save if the ball misses or glances off the stick.

8.1.5 High

As you might have guessed, you still need to step to the ball on high shots. Here are a few more comments.

8.1.5.1   Stick-side High

The two most common mistakes on stick-side high shots are:

1) <u>Not stepping to the ball:</u> The ball nicks the wall and bounces in easily, because the goalie's body isn't aligned with the shot. If you're right-handed and a high shot is coming, step out to it with your right foot and then immediately step with your back (left) foot.

116

2) <u>Punching out at the ball:</u> The stick-side high shot may seem simple to save, but in the heat of the battle, the goalie can get wound pretty tight and have a hard time "softening" his hands. For some reason, this seems to happen a lot on these shots, as the goalie goes into tennis racket mode. The key is to practice a lot, even though the shot seems easy to save.

Figure 8-11 – Basic Stick-side High save move

8.1.5.2   *Off-side High*

This one can be hard, especially if the shooter can hit that top far corner. The standard move is to quickly flip the stickhead across your face. But this raises a problem: If the shot is a "tweener" – somewhere between off-side hip and offside high, should the goalie use the across-the-face move or the same move as for offside hip?

Figure 8-12 – Basic Offside High save move

The general rule of thumb is that if the shot is higher than 5 inches or so above your waist, go across the face. If lower, use the usual offside hip move. This will vary from goalie to goalie, so you have to find what works best for you. In my case, I'm probably worse at the across-the-face move than at the other, so I use the across-the-face only on the highest shots (approximately armpit level and above). But I've seen goalies who were great at getting across their face, even on shots as low as the waist. Have somebody throw a lot of these shots at you and see which is better. Then practice it so it becomes automatic.

Figure 8-13 – Basic Offside High save move

8.1.5.3   *Straight*

When a 90 mph shot comes right at your face, the natural reflex is to duck – for most normal people. But goalies have to be different. If you're new to the game, don't worry – getting hit in the facemask doesn't hurt. This is an improvement over a helmet I had back in the 1960's. The facemask had no vertical bar in the middle – one day a hard shot bent the horizontal bars apart, so that the ball went through the mask and broke my nose.

You just have to train yourself to stand there. Of course, ideally, you'll step to the ball, get your stick over and make a clean save. As with the hip-high shot straight at the midsection, the main problem I've seen on straight high shots is not stepping to the ball.

Jumping

In general, jumping for a high shot is a bad idea and isn't successful. If you're in position, you can reach any shot without jumping - by stepping to the ball and using your stick. If scouts or game film show that you jump at high shots a lot, a decent opponent will use this against you by faking high and shooting low.

There are a couple qualified exceptions:

1) If you get a late look at a high shot or if you know you can't get your stick to it (say, on an offside high shot), then your last resort may be to spring up and try to get hit in the shoulder. I've made an embarrassing number of saves like this (embarrassing because my stick couldn't get to the shot in time), but it's really a last resort move. See Figure 8-14 below:

Figure 8-14 – Like I said…don't jump

Comments: *Here's a picture of me, caught in the act, and guilty as charged. In summary, I jumped like a jackrabbit, trying to get my shoulder in the way of an offside high shot. I'd have been better off stepping to the ball and using the across-the-face move for the offside high shot – but I guess made the split second decision that I couldn't get my stick there in time, so would try to get the shoulder there. Turned out this was a bad decision, as the shot went in.*

2) If you're out of the crease chasing a loose ball, the opponent comes up with it and makes a quick feed out front, and the only way for you to get any chance at all of stopping the shot with your stick or some body part, then it's ok to dive at the crease and hope you get in the way. This doesn't work too often, but is better than doing nothing.

8.1.6 When They Score

In all my years in the goal, I've only tossed three shutouts, all against teams that weren't very good. In other words, goalies get scored on, and they get scored on in every game.

So…what to do when the worst happens – I make a move on the ball, even a good one, but it goes in. I'm not happy, to say the least – I really hate to get scored on. But here's how I try to shake it off, learn from any mistake I might have made, and get my head back in the game.

1) First, the ref wants to ball, so I just rake it out of the goal and toss it to him. No matter how mad I am, it doesn't do any good to heave it downfield in anger. I did that once a long time ago and hit one of my teammates smack in the helmet. Not good. So that was the last time I pulled that stunt.

2) Next, what do I say to my D-men? To repeat, here's what I wrote in Section 1.1.1:

> Here's what I do: If I think the guy knows what he did wrong, I just say something like, "Hey no sweat, Joe, you'll get him next time."
>
> If I feel he needs to think about what he messed up, I'll say, "OK, what happened?" Then he has to think about it, analyze at least a little bit, and come up with an answer. Usually, he'll know exactly what went wrong and will say, "Yeah, I was slow to move with him" or "I overcommitted too soon." Then I'll say, "OK, you'll get him next time."
>
> If he has no clue what he did wrong, then I'll have to tell him what he did wrong and what he should have done – not in a mean sarcastic way – I just try to be firm, plain and direct. If he never gets better, keeps making the same mistakes over and over, and/or has a bad attitude, then I suggest talking with your coach – in private – and asking him to give somebody else a chance.

3) Next, I have to get myself straightened out. Once a goal is scored, I have to forget about it, because there's still a lot of game left to play. There's no point in beating myself up too much if the goal was my fault. I don't dwell on it. Instead, here's what I do:

    a) <u>Rework the muscle memory:</u> If the shot went by me on offside low, then I practice that move several times, starting slowly and going full speed by the fifth rep or so. That gets my muscle memory back in shape for that move, and also helps me get my head back in the game.

    b) <u>Talk to myself:</u> I take a deep breath, tell myself "OK, that one's gone. Get back in the game. I'll get the next one."

    c) <u>Back to Basics:</u> I review my stance, from the feet up, as I've described in Section 5.2, remind myself to watch the ball, and pay attention to the face-off. When a goalie's head gets out of joint, his mechanics start to frazzle. So conversely, by focusing on making sure your mechanics are in good shape, you get your head back where it needs to be.

8.2   Passing and Catching

Passing and catching mistakes cost teams ballgames. Every time you turn the ball over, you're giving the opponent a chance to score. Conversely, if you can take care of the ball, you have a much better chance of clearing, controlling the ball, scoring and winning.

Just for the heck of it, the next time you watch a game, count the bad passes and missed catches. My guess is that the team with the most turnovers will lose the game.

Passing and catching well are so basic to lacrosse that, strangely, they sometimes get ignored, as people start to spend all their time on complicated defense packages, tricky behind-the-back shots, and offensive plays that make quantum physics look like basic math.

The best players – including the best goalies - have great fundamentals. They make accurate passes that are not too hard, too soft, too high or too low. They can throw a lead pass that hits a teammate who's running full speed downfield. They catch every ball within reach, and some that are way off target. They can pass and catch equally well – or almost equally well – with both hands.

How did they get so good? The answer is simple: Practice. This book can't really teach you how to throw and catch, but I'll mention a few things that might help.

8.2.1 Catching

In some ways, making saves is just an advanced form of catching. So if you practice plain old ordinary catching, it can help you make clean saves and control the ball, even on the hardest shots.

Furthermore, when you're clearing the ball, you'll need to pass and catch well. Goalies obviously don't want to be throwing bad passes in the defensive end of the field. More on clearing in Section 10.0, but it all starts with good stickwork.

A couple of things to remember about catching:

- Show your stickhead to your teammate who has the ball – hold it up in "the box" (just to the side of your head) where he can see it. He needs a target.

- To be ready to catch a pass, I hold my top hand right next to the head of the stick, with my bottom hand about 24 inches down the shaft. If the pass is high, I can quickly loosen the top hand and shoot my stickhead up with the lower hand. If the pass is low, I'm ready to go into "save" mode: step to the ball and get the stickhead down, just like making a save.

- I recommend practicing catching with both hands. You never know when you'll need to put your body between a defender and your stickhead and "show" your stick to your offside.

- When an opponent is riding your teammate hard, and he needs to get rid of the ball, make sure you "show" for him – meaning run to a spot where there's no opponent between him and you, so that he has an open passing lane to you.

8.2.2 Passing

Throwing a lacrosse ball isn't that hard, but throwing a perfect pass every time is.

If you're a complete beginner, then I recommend you get with a good coach who can give you a hands-on lesson. Just a couple of basics:

- Hand position: Unlike in catching, put your lower hand (left hand when throwing righty) down on or near the butt end of the shaft and your top hand (right hand when passing righty) about a forearm's length above it. This will vary from person to person, but the main point is that, unlike catching, when you pass, you seldom want your top hand right near the stickhead. If you have your top hand too far close to the stickhead, the pass will usually go too low.

- Long passes: The farther you have to throw, the farther down the shaft you slide the top hand – up to a point, of course. I've seldom thrown a pass with my hands less than 12 or 14 inches apart.

- Passing from a standing (not running) position: This is the easiest pass to make. Unless necessary, I don't normally face my whole body fully in the direction I'm throwing. If throwing right-handed, turn your left shoulder toward the target, give the ball a little cradle so you can feel where it is in the stick, "wind up" by having the stick about parallel to the ground, step with your left foot directly at the target, and throw. It's a pretty natural movement, so shouldn't be too hard. If you're having a problem, try this: pull down and back with your left hand, and push while snapping the wrist a little with the right. I used this technique to teach myself to throw lefty, so you might want to give it a try.

- Follow through: Usually, the farther you have to throw, the longer the follow-through. For short passes, you can sometimes just give it a quick "pop" with very little follow-through.
  - Passes too high?: If you find that your passes are too high, then you're probably not following through enough, or your throwing motion is taking too long, or your top hand is too far down toward the butt end of the shaft, or your pocket is too tight.

o <u>Passes too low?:</u> If your passes are going too low, then decrease your follow through, slow down your throwing motion, move your top hand toward the butt end, and/or tighten up your pocket.

- <u>Release Point:</u> Note that every stick has a different "ideal release point," i.e., the spot on the mesh where you want the ball to come off of when you pass. On a goalie stick, this is usually in the center of the mesh, about 4 inches down from the top edge of the stick-wall. This'll be different if you have shooting strings, and also depends on how deep your pocket is. You just have to practice until you can take that quick cradle and go back just far enough to "set" the ball in the right spot before you throw. Practice a lot – and when you're playing catch or wall ball, don't just fling the ball around: Pick a specific spot to aim for – a brick in the wall, your buddy's stickhead, whatever.

- <u>Passing while running:</u> The basics are the same as when you're standing still – if at all possible, give it a cradle, cock, step, throw, follow through. When running, it's a little harder to make a full follow-through. But if you find that your passes on the run are going high, then you'll need to find out why: it could be that your follow-through is too short, or that the ball is releasing from too high up in the mesh.

When I pass on the run, I often throw three-quarters or sidearm. This lets me get the ball off more quickly than using a full overhand wind-up.

You have to practice passing on the run a lot. Start slow, jogging, with short passes, and gradually build up to faster speeds and longer passes. I recommend doing this every day.

- <u>Aspects and Types of Passes:</u> Whether you're running or passing from a set position, there are a few different types of passes a goalie has to learn to throw. Passes vary mainly in the following areas:

o <u>Distance:</u> You have to be able to throw accurately anywhere from 5 to 50 or 60 yards.

o <u>Speed of release:</u> Sometimes you need to get the ball off instantly, for example, when an opponent is about to nail you. In this case you have to be able to cock and deliver fast. You usually can't throw this pass too far (maybe 20 yards, depending on your skill level), but it's better to get it off at least in the general direction of your teammate, than to get hit and lose the ball. You'll usually be running when you have to get the ball off fast, so you can practice this by just running up the field with a teammate 10 or 15 yards away.

o <u>Sidearm? Overhand? What should I do?:</u> Like baseball pitchers, you can throw a lacrosse ball straight overhand, "three quarters," sidearm or even underhand. Which is better? The quick answer is "Practice from all angles, because sooner or later, you'll need to throw all of them." In general, for long passes, I throw more straight overhand or close to it, especially if I'm not rushed. I can get more distance when needed, and also have time to set, cock, step and follow through.

Figure 8-15 – Overhand Pass – Side View: The Wind-up
Note: Especially for new goalies – when you "wind up," keep your stick level, parallel to the ground. Lots of new goalies wind up too far, i.e., let the stickhead drop down too far. The ball falls out of the mesh and sometimes right into the goal. I even saw a D1 goalie do this once – very embarrassing, and doesn't help your team when you score on yourself.

Figure 8-16 – Overhand Pass – Side View: Stepping as you throw

Figure 8-17 – Overhand Pass – Side View: The follow-through

Figure 8-18 – Overhand Pass – Front View: The Wind-up

In general, you want to point your shoulder at your target, look at your man, and step toward the target. This is a basic, solid approach that I still use unless I have to reach into the bag of tricks. Stick with the fundamentals until you get good enough to throw off-balance, look one way and throw another, fake one way and throw another, and things like that.

Figure 8-19 – Overhand Pass – Front View: The follow-through

The overhand pass works well in most situations, but for the quick, shorter passes, as mentioned above, I go three-quarters or even sidearm (see Figures 8-20 and 8-21 below) - especially if I'm on the run. I throw underhand (or even backhanded) if it's my only option for getting the ball past an opponent who's riding me tight. Practice all four, but mainly the first two: Overhand and three-quarters.

Figure 8-20 – Sidearm Pass, Part 1 – The "Windup"

Figure 8-21 – Sidearm Pass, Part 2 – The Follow-through
Note that even when throwing sidearm, I still step toward the target with my offside foot.

o **Speed:** When passing, you usually don't want to throw as hard as you can because the 80 mph pass is harder for your teammate to catch. On the other hand, you often have only a split second to get the ball to, say, a breaking middie, before an opponent covers him. So you have to practice putting some juice on the ball, but not making like it's a hard shot contest. Normally, your short and mid-range toss (10 to 25 yards) should have some arc, but not be a rainbow.

o **Touch Pass:** On the other hand, when a middie is breaking downfield, you often have to throw a mid-range to long (25 – 40 yards) "touch pass" that he can run under and catch, just like a receiver in football going for the "timing" pass in the corner of the end zone. It's important to get really good at this type of pass, and the only way I know to do it is practice.

There are a couple things that your teammates can do to make these passes successful more often. Share these ideas with them and practice as much as you can:

1) When your teammate breaks, it's best if he heads in a straight line. If he's weaving down the field, it's hard for you to pick a point ahead of him to pass to, where he and the pass will arrive at the same time.

2) It's best if he maintains the same speed while he's breaking. As soon as he gets up to about full speed, he shouldn't start downshifting and then upshifting unpredictably.

3) The breaker needs to turn his head and look at the goalie right away. The keeper has only 4 seconds to either throw or get out of the crease, so running and looking straight downfield for too long won't help.

Of course, these guidelines aren't hard and fast, as the breaker might have to change speeds or break right or left if an opponent shows up. But if he has a clean break after a save, he should keep these things in mind: Run straight, at the same speed, while looking for the pass.

You'll often need to throw this pass right after you make a save. I'll talk more about this in *Section 10.0 - Clearing*, but here's a place where being able to throw straight overhand and three-quarters can be important. After the save, there's usually an opponent standing there, waving his stick, trying to block my pass: If his stick is out to the side, my straight overhand throw will shoot right over his head. If his stick is right above his head, then I can go three-quarters, and whip it past his shoulder. You have to make this judgment fast, so it's really important to be good at both the straight overhead and the three-quarters passes. I even go sidearm in some cases, so feel free to practice that as well, after you've mastered overhand and three-quarters.

o **The Buddy Pass:** If you haven't heard this term, it means throwing a pass to a teammate who is closely guarded and who will get creamed just as he catches the ball. You won't make many friends on your team if you throw more than one of these a season. So make sure your man is open before you step and throw.

- ○ <u>Backhanded Pass:</u> Due to lots of hours of goofing off and (some might say) wasting my time when I could have been doing something useful, I can toss it backhanded if I get desperate. But I haven't really needed it very often – maybe once a season or so. Until you get really good at all the standard passes, and if your practice time is limited, I wouldn't recommend worrying about the backhanded pass much. On the other hand, it's fun to do when you're messing around, and if you play long enough, you'll need it some day, so go for it when you have some down time.

- ▪ <u>Go Left and Right:</u> I think that a goalie ought to learn to throw, catch and scoop with both hands. You don't have to be great with your off-hand, but it'll be helpful to at least be able to throw a short pass. I admit I'm a little different in that I'm a natural right-hander in passing, but for some reason have always felt more comfortable playing lefty in the goal. Bottom line is that I taught myself to throw lefty, and it's been really useful over the years. For example, when clearing the ball, and pressure comes from my right side, I can always switch to my left hand and pass out to that side. Or in an unsettled situation, if I need to scoop, I can do that with either hand, and then head whichever way keeps my body between my stick and an opponent. Or when I make a save and there's an opponent on the right side of the crease, I can switch to my left hand and make the outlet pass before he can get over to guard that side.

I never saw much advantage to playing both right and left when setting up to make saves, but a few guys do it. I think if you're a good right- or left-handed goalie, you should be able to get to just about any shot, and that turning around the other way probably wouldn't have helped to make the save.

The exception might be playing right-handed on the right pipe and left-handed on the left pipe, which could help cut off the high inside-pipe shot - but you have to make sure you can get the stickhead across to save the offside high shot too. You're welcome to try it if you like.

The other small possibility is that you'll have an experience like mine: I started out as a right-hander, but in the course of practicing my left hand, I found that I did better in the cage lefty than righty. I can't explain this, and I think it's fairly rare – but it's worth checking out if you have the time and inclination.

9.0 Talk - Running the Defense

Other than the basic ball location calls mentioned below in Section 9.1, the goalie needs to talk about a lot of other things. Exactly what words you use and what you say in different situations will depend, again, on:

a) what works best for you and your defense, and
b) what defensive packages your coach puts in.

Regardless of the details of Items a and b, there are a few basic things you have to tell your defense and some good ways to do it.

1. Ball Location
2. Loudness
3. "Chatter" and Slide Calls
4. Check
5. Clearing

9.1 Ball Location

This section is mainly for new goalies, but I'll add a few thoughts that might help even the guys with a couple years in the cage.

Calling out ball location: What can be hard about that? Well, it's not hard, but let's go over the basics.

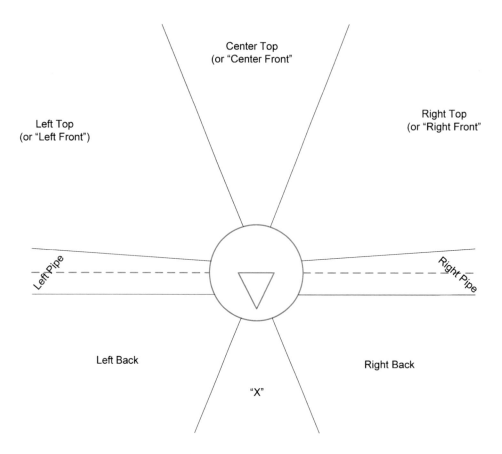

Figure 9-1 – Ball Location

The main locations are:
- Left Top (some say "Left Front" instead of "Left Top")
- Center Top (or just "Center") or Center Front
- Right Top or Right Front
- Right Pipe
- Left Pipe
- Right Back
- Left Back
- X (Center Back)

There is some debate over whether a goalie should say "Left Top" or "Top Left". Some recommend saying the direction first ("<u>Left</u> Top") because that at least tells your teammates which side of the field the ball is on (when they can't see it, which is often).

Also, if the ball is at Left Back, it kind of flows better if you say "Left Back," then "Left Pipe," and then "Left Top," which is a fairly common sequence, e.g., if the ballhandler carries the ball himself, or if he starts to pass it around the perimeter. This might help your long-sticks to more easily visualize where the ball is moving.

Others think it's more important to get out the "Top" part first. Some think it really doesn't matter that much. <u>My view is that the goalie and defenders need to talk it over before the season, see what works best for them, and then stick with it unless it causes some problems.</u>

9.2   *Loudness*

I'm always surprised when I watch a game and can barely hear the goalie. If I can't hear him from 50 yards away, then I suspect that his D-men aren't hearing enough either. I've seen goalies who had great saving skills but just never said much to their defense, which caused them to have to use those skills more than they should have had to! Don't be afraid to yell.

<u>Early in a game, after the first time the opponent has had the ball, I always ask my D-men if they can hear me all right</u>. If not, I turn up the volume until they can.

It's a good idea to vary your loudness and speed. If you just talk at the same volume and cadence the whole time, your D-men might not know when things are getting hairy. My normal volume is loud enough for them to hear, but if an attackman is coming around the corner and I need a defender to slide, I'll yell "Slide! Slide!" really loud and fast. Before a game I'll tell my defense – including middies - "OK, when you hear me starting to scream, pay attention, cuz that means somebody is heading for the goal."

9.3   *"Chatter"*

Chatter is just the stuff you say to your defenders during the normal course of playing D. Most of this talk is directed at the guy guarding the ballhandler. Remember that your D-man has his back to the goal most of the time, especially when guarding a guy with the ball, and often has no clue about how dangerously close his attackman is getting to an easy shot. So you have to keep telling him where he is and what to do.

When there's little danger of an easy shot, then I'll just say, "Jim, you're good, you're good," or "You're good, he's way out there," – while still calling out the ball location "Right Back" or whatever, so that everybody else can hear it.

As the ballhandler starts to come in and get in a more dangerous position, I'll yell something like "Jim, get on him, poke him. He's getting close," or whatever code you've agreed a head of time. We used to say, "Give him some wood," but there aren't any wooden sticks these days, and "Give him some plastic" doesn't really do much for me.

As the attacker moves in, I'll start to get the "slider" ready – usually by yelling "Who's hot?" ("Hot" being the usual term for "the guy who has to slide first") - or by telling the closest defender – "Bill, you're hot." What you say will depend on your defensive packages, but the main point is that when you see a defender looking like he's about to

133

get beat, or if you're calling early slides, you need to yell out whatever code word you have to tell the slider to move. For example, I've seen people use any word starting with "E" – like eat, enter, elbow – to stand for "early slide." This particular "code" might be a little too easy for your opponent to figure out, but you can use whatever works for you.

Before each game, I also set up a code word that means "The guy is about to shoot, so for crying out loud, somebody get over there and slow him down, nail him, check him, hit him." I don't want to yell out all that or even let the shooter know he's *that* open, by saying something like "He's got a shot," so I use a word like "Hit" or "Fire." Anything is ok, as long as it's one syllable and your D-men know what to do.

9.4 "Check"

This is usually about the first thing a goalie learns to yell, so probably not much need for elaboration. For you new guys, when a feeder gets off a pass that looks like an attacker can catch and shoot, just yell "Check!" Everybody on your team needs to know that this means – "Hit the nearest attacker's stick – NOW." It's a key aspect of playing defense, but I still see goalies who don't yell it and defenders who don't actually check any sticks when they hear it.

9.5 Clearing

Talking before and during the clear is important, and I'll cover this in *Section 10.0*.

9.6 Loose Ball

So there you are, in your stance, talking away, ball is Left Top, and all of a sudden a miracle occurs: The attacker drops the ball. Before the game, you tell your guys what you'll yell in this situation: "Ball down – Left Top" or whatever. As I mentioned in Section 6.3.2, if the attacker drops the ball and doesn't know it, don't yell out "Ball down" instantly. Wait until he's run for a couple more strides (cradling air all the way) so that he's away from the ball. You can then yell "Ball down" – the D-man on the ballhandler might already know this, but the rest of your defense is probably looking elsewhere. They need to turn and look, and be ready to break for a pass if your teammate gets the ground ball.

9.6.1 General Approach to Loose Balls

If we get the loose ball, then you need to start directing the clear. A lot of times, the situation is so unsettled that you won't be going into some pre-set clear play, but your defenders should still use the same principles as on a clear: keep spread out, break for open space, tell your man where you are. A lot of guys have a code word or weird yelping noise they make when they're open. Use whatever works, just so that everybody knows the plan.

What often happens on a loose ball is that all your D-men and middies decide to run out there and try to get it. As goalie, you have to tell at least one guy to stay back in the "Hole" (the area right in front of the crease). Before the game, make sure your D-men and middies understand what you mean when you yell, "Jack, get the hole." See Figure 9-2 below:

Figure 9-2 – Loose Ball Top Center

Comment: Goalie tells his D-man (the white jersey next to the crease, in the center of the picture) to get the hole. Note that there are two attackers – one to the right of the crease, and one to the left – who can get open for an easy shot if the opponent gets the ball. In this case, the goalie might tell another D-man to drop back and guard the left crease area.

When the ball is down, some goalies have a tendency to relax and get lazy – just because the attacker doesn't have possession. But the best thing to do is stay in position on the arc and maintain a good "ready to save" stance. See Figure 9-3 below: There was a loose ball right in front of the cage. The goalie is still in his "ready to save" stance and still on the right spot on the arc. His D-man has just scooped the ball, but the goalie stays ready, just in case the opponent checks his teammate's stick and knocks the ball loose again.

Figure 9-3 – Loose Ball but Goalie stays ready

The one exception to maintaining my "ready to save" stance is that when the ball is on the ground, I'll usually lower my stickhead down farther than usual. I do this because a lot of attackers will scoop up a loose ball and immediately fling an underhand shot from about 6 or 12 inches above the ground. Youth league and some high school kids might not have this shot in their repertoire, but I saw it a lot in college and still see it in club ball all the time. See Figure 9-4 below:

Figure 9-4 – Goalie is lowering stickhead down to be in line with height of loose ball.

Hopefully your defender will scoop up the loose ball, run downfield and toss it to our attackman. But if he gets turned back, then the goalie needs to start setting up and running the clear (see *Section 10.0*).

If we don't get the loose ball, then the goalie has to get the defense to re-set asap. Again, have a predetermined word or phrase for this situation. I usually just yell, "Defense - set up – get a man," and keep yelling until things settle down.

If I'm feeling ornery, and think the attackers have a chance to take advantage of our not being ready yet, then I'll change my voice and yell something like "OK, work it around one time. Slow it down. Settle the ball." You'd be surprised at how often this works. The attack "obeys" me, slows it down, and starts tossing passes around the perimeter. This gives us time to find our men and re-set the D.

9.6.2 Raking

When a shot rebounds out front, and you can get to it before anybody else, reach out, clamp, and rake it back into the crease. As you do this, keep your back foot (usually the left foot if you're right-handed) inside the crease. That way, you can go completely back into the crease a) after you get control of the ball, or b) as you're raking. If you come out once, and then go back in, that's a re-entry (or "in and out") penalty, and the opponent gets possession. See Figure 9-5 below:

Figure 9-5 – Raking back into the Crease
Notice the goalie keeping his left foot in the crease, so that he can stay in the crease once he gets control of the ball.

- When raking just be careful that you don't lose control of the ball and rake it back into the goal. It's hard enough to keep the other guys from scoring, without putting it in all by yourself.
- If you clamp the ball in the crease, and an attackman or two are whacking at your stick, keep your mesh flat to the ground and try to turn your butt toward them (without leaving the crease). Putting your body between them and the ball will give you a better chance of doing a clean rake.

9.6.3 Scooping

A goalie needs to be able to scoop just as well as a middie. Here are some basic things to remember (assuming you're scooping right-handed):

1) About 4 or 5 feet from the ball, I get down as low as I can. This means getting my rear end down low, bending over, and lowering my stick so it's almost parallel to the ground, with the butt end about 6 or 8 inches above the grass.

2) I try to size my steps so that when I reach the ball, my right foot is right next to the ball or just 6 to 8 inches behind the ball, about a foot or so to the right of the path the ball is rolling in. This takes some practice, but becomes natural after you've done it a few hundred times.

3) Just before I reach the ball, as I take that last step, I get down even lower, so that I can scoop the ball. As with anything in lacrosse, it's critical to keep your eye on the ball. On ground balls, there are usually a lot of distractions, like opponents whacking at you, but you have to ignore all this, maintain your solid technique, watch the ball, and scoop through it..

Figure 9-6 – Scooping: Side View

Note: Bend knees, left foot next to stickhead (when playing left-handed), get low on the ball.

Figure 9-7 – Scooping: ¾ Front View

Note: Bend knees, right foot next to stickhead (when playing right-handed), get low on the ball.

Figure 9-8 – Scooping: Front View

Note: Bend knees, left foot next to stickhead (when playing left-handed), get low on the ball. My right hand should probably be even lower.

4) As I scoop the ball, I keep both hands on the stick, and then draw the stick close to my body, going into a cradle and protecting the ball with my body as I come up. Protecting the stick is especially critical for goalies, since our stick is big and makes a nice target.

5) I know a lot of people scoop with just one hand on the stick these days. They say that the game is so fast that they don't have time to slow down and scoop the old-

fashioned way (i.e., what I just described). There may be some truth to this for short sticks, but I still see a lot of them missing the one-handed scoop, which looks pretty lame.

One-handed is even harder with a goalie stick, because of the additional length and weight. If you want to try one-handed scoops, fine, but you'd better be really strong, so you can control the stickhead throughout the scoop, and also be able to protect the stick instantly after making the scoop. I've found it's easier to just get down low, keep both hands on the stick, and drive through the scoop. It helps that I practice running as fast as I can while bent over. Go as fast and low as you can during scooping drills – you won't regret it.

6) In summary, I suggest you try it my way first. If you have weak legs and/or thighs, you might not be able to get down very far, but that's all the more reason to build up your legs in your conditioning program. You're going to need them for making saves anyway, so no sense in delaying the inevitable, right?

See Figure 9-9 below: This is what happens to goalies who don't bend down all the way to scoop the ball. Note also that the goalie didn't step with his right foot next to the ball, so his body isn't between the ball and the opponent – this also leaves his big goalie stick unprotected. The White Jersey had an easy time checking the goalie's stick and eventually got the loose ball.

Figure 9-9 – How not to Scoop

10.0 Clearing

I think some people underestimate how important clears are. This includes players, coaches and fans. They focus on things like goals, assists, saves, face-offs, penalties and ground balls - and sometimes you'll see clearing stats at the bottom of the boxscore.

But clears are just as important as face-offs, penalties and ground balls – they all either get the ball into your attacking end, or keep you on defense. In some ways, the clear is even more important because you should be able to clear <u>every time</u> – while face-offs and ground balls often depend on which way the ball happens to bounce. On a clear, the D has its success or failure in its own hands – all the guys have to do is work the clear play, throw good passes, get open, catch the ball, and run.   On a clear, you outnumber the bad guys 7 to 6, so getting somebody open should be doable.

10.1 What not to Do

During a couple of my club leagues, I usually got to the field early and watched a couple of high school or other club games. The skill level was fairly high, but I was always shocked at how nonchalantly a lot of the goalies and D-men approached their clears. Goalies often just winged the ball downfield in the general direction of a teammate, whether the guy was covered or not.   D-men weren't spreading out to avoid the single-rider-covering-two-defenders problem.   Overall I'd say the clear rate was about 50%.

OK, it was "just summer league," but it still wasn't good lacrosse. If you have a choice and know how to clear right, why choose to be sloppy and let the other team have the ball? You wouldn't pass it to them on purpose, would you?

10.2 Clear Packages

So…following that rant, here are a few words about clearing.

First, every coach will put in clears, and the goalie will need to learn them and be able to work them. Each clear will require different skills of the goalie, so you'll need to practice whatever is needed. For example, you might need to make a long pass across the field, so work on your long passes. You might need to run with the ball to force the 2-on-1, so run those wind sprints and make sure your cradling is good.

I'm not going to preach that any one clear is better than another. Your coach will decide that based on his experience and on your team's strengths and weaknesses. But I will say that there are a few basic principles that hold true for just about any clear:

10.3 Clear off the Save

First, in my mind, the goalie is in charge of setting up and running the clear – which means that he has to yell at everybody to tell them what to do.

When you make a save and control the ball in the crease, yell "Break" or some other code word, to let your defenders know that you've got the ball and are looking for an outlet pass right away. If they're not cutting downfield already, "Break" should set them off, and you can then look for a pass.

Figure 10-1 – Goalie makes save, yells "Break," looks for outlet pass
Note: He's looking downfield first, to try for the quick break, but has a D-man as a "safety valve" on his right (the white jersey on the far left of the photo).

"Look for a pass": Sounds pretty easy, right? The main problem goalies have is tunnel vision. They look right, and if nobody's open out there, they don't have time to look left. You have 4 seconds to either pass or get out of the crease, so you need to be able to see the whole field, pick out your open cutter, and throw the ball before time's up. I'm not sure I can "teach" a goalie how to have this type of vision. I suspect there are exercises that can help, and I'm sure people claim they can help, but I don't know enough about it to make a sensible judgment.

Figure 10-2 – Outlet Pass

Comment: This old (about 1977) photo shows what I'm talking about. I've just made the save, looked up and scanned the field quickly, and found an open man to pass to – before these three goons can collapse on me. The sticks and helmets may look out of date, but the principles have stayed the same.

The best advice I can offer you on this is to <u>practice trying to see the whole field</u>. That may sound simplistic, but it's better than practicing 'looking in only one direction'. I've tried to analyze what's happening right after I make a save and start looking for the open man: In summary, it's a different type of "seeing" than when I'm focusing hard on watching the ball in a shooter's stick. When looking for the outlet pass, my eyes kind of give the field a quick "sweep" and can pick out the guy in the right-colored jersey who's running downfield. This sweep only takes a second. Give it a try and see if it improves your ability to pick out the cutter.

Another thing you can do is stand out of bounds behind the goal when somebody else is playing a game or even 6 on 6. Look over to the left and see if you can pick out what's going on to the right, and vice versa. Gradually, you'll start seeing more and more of what's happening everywhere on the field. And, finally, the more you play, the better you'll get at seeing what's going on on most of the field.

Figure 10-3 – Look downfield, but be aware of what's going on to the right and left
Comments: Goalie has just made a save and is looking downfield for the outlet pass. If nobody gets open downfield, then he has to be aware that he has a safety valve to his left. It takes practice to develop the vision to know where everybody is.
Note that on most clear plays, one D-man needs to break to the right wing, one to the left, and the other should break downfield, toward the left or right sideline, on a 45 degree angle from the goal.

If you go to http://www.lacrosse.org/pdf/findspace1.pdf, you'll find an article called *Finding Space* by Kevin Sheehan, who has coached successfully for many years. This includes drills that should help a goalie see the field better and find the open man (plus lots of other skills for non-goalies). I'm sure there are other drills, and I expect that your coach will know some.

10.4 Dead Ball Clear

When clearing from a dead ball situation, the goalie has to tell everybody what clear you're going into. Most teams have code words (Blue, Red, Ford, Chevy, whatever) to tell the defenders what clear is on. When the defense gets to start a clear at X, the goalie will usually take the ball and get things going. As the clear develops and the riders start to make their moves, the goalie will make the first pass, and things continue to develop from there.

Since I've always played a lot of club ball, we seldom have any complicated clears in place and never have any practice time. If you find yourself in this situation, then I've found that the simplest dead ball clear, which usually works pretty well, goes like this:

1) Goalie takes the dead ball in the middle of the field, either in front of or behind the cage.

2) Two D-men are parallel to the goalie, one near the left sideline, one near the right sideline.

3) Third D-man is in front of one of these guys (either left or right – doesn't matter). He's half-way between the D-man and his own middie, who is closer to midfield.

4) Middies are spread out across the field (one middle, one right, one left), also more or less parallel to each other. They start about 15 yards or so from the midfield stripe, in the defensive end of the field.

5) Your attackmen should be 5 yards or so back from midfield, and should gradually work their way back toward the goal they're shooting at, as we move the ball up toward midfield. This is really important, because a lot of times the attackers stay right at midfield, which causes all our guys to be jammed too close together as the ball nears midfield.

See Figure 10-4 below for a diagram of the basic dead-ball clear set-up.

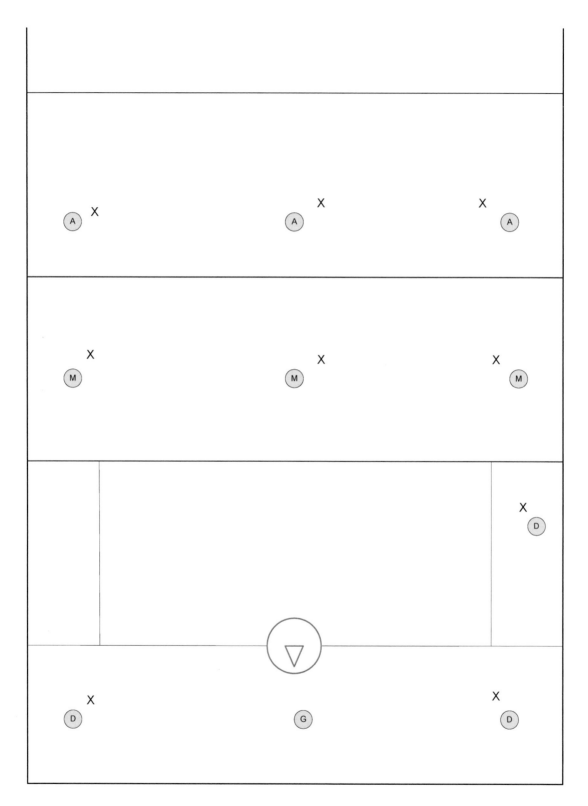

Figure 10-4 – Dead Ball Clear Set-up
(Opponents are the X's)

146

6) Usually the riders will have their 3 middies on our 3 middies, and their 3 attackers trying to cover the goalie and our 3 D-men. In this case, I just head right or left (hopefully toward their least athletic attacker), and force the 2 on 1: i.e., so there's only one of them trying to guard me and my D-man. The attacker will usually jump the goalie, who then throws a perfect pass to his open D-man, who then either runs it over the midline, or works his own 2 on 1. See Figure 10-5 below.

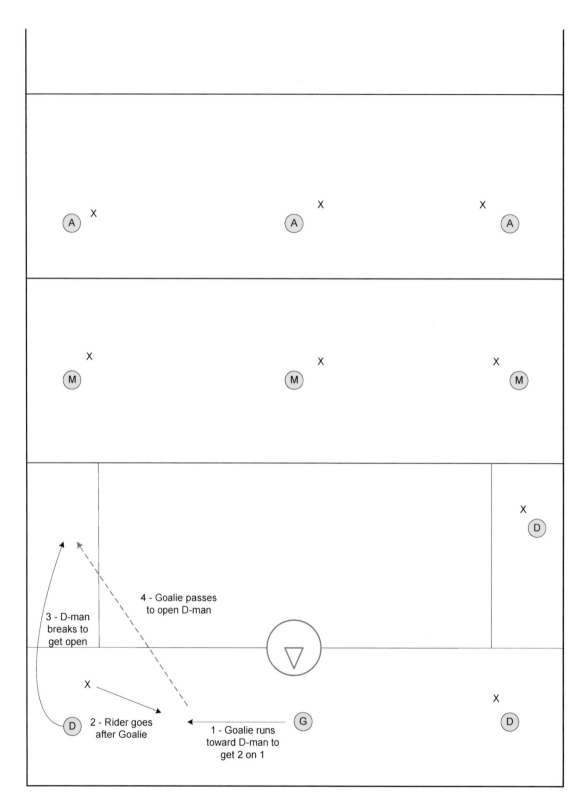

Figure 10-5 – Simple Dead Ball Clear – Forcing the 2 on 1

A couple of points:

1) "Show for me": Before the game, make sure that your D-man knows that he has to "show" for you in this situation. That means that he can't let the rider who jumps you be directly between you and the D-man. He has to break either left or right to give you a clear passing lane.

2) Trail the play and stay open: After the goalie makes the pass, he needs to make sure he's open in case the D-man gets jumped (for example, by a riding middie who's speeding down on him). Tell your D-man: "I'm open if you need me." He's looking downfield but can tell more or less where you are from your voice – plus he needs to know that he still has an option to throw back to you if he doesn't have any other choices.

*Don't bunch up: Note again that if the D-man, who now has the ball, turns and starts downfield, this is when it really gets important for our attackmen to drop back toward the goal they're shooting at, so they don't clog things up in the midfield area. As goalie, I always remind them of this before a game, and start yelling at them to get back when my D-man takes off. See Figure 10-6 below:

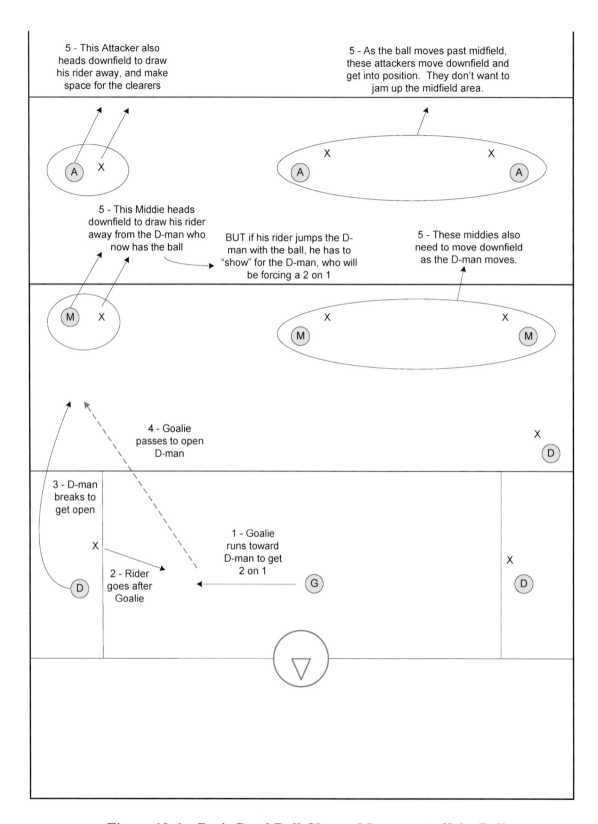

Figure 10-6 – Basic Dead Ball Clear – Movement off the Ball

The clear shown in Figures 10-4 to 10-6 (above) is pretty simple and surprisingly effective. I've been doing it for years with decent success. Usually it breaks down only because of a bad pass or dropped ball.

There are a lot of variations, of course. For example, see Figure 10-7 below: If the riders use one of their 6 men to guard the goalie, which leaves a middie open downfield, then you have to decide what to do. One option is for the Goalie to yell out a code that means "Press ride. I'm covered. Whoever the unguarded Middie is needs to get down here asap so I can pass to him."

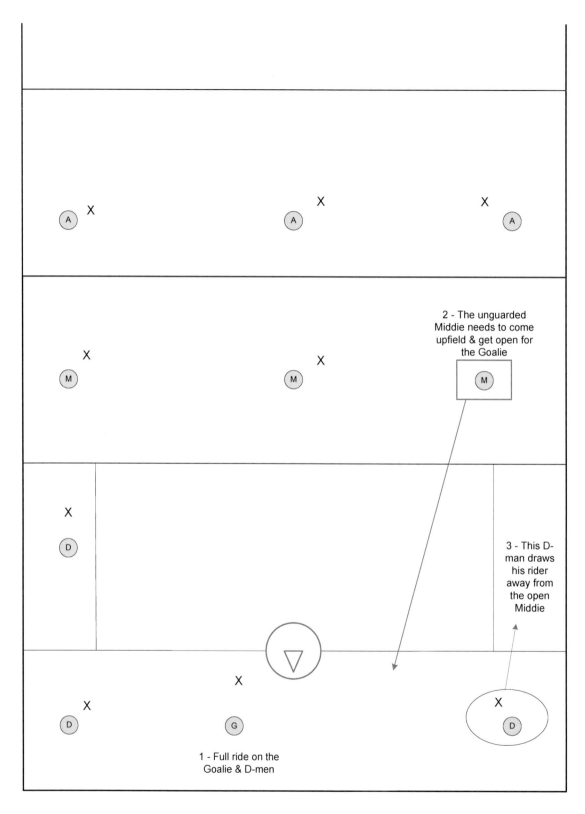

Figure 10-7 – Handling the Full Press Ride

152

Other options: The goalie can try to dodge, or you can bring the free middie down to take the dead ball before the whistle blows. Middies are usually better dodgers than goalies, so this is almost always the best approach. Pick your best dodger, who hopefully also has good speed: At the whistle he has 5 yards between himself and the rider, so should be able to get by, run downfield and look for a 2 on 1 - or just take it all the way.

10.5 Clearing up the Middle

I try to avoid clearing up the middle of the field. If I throw into the middle and my guy drops the pass or I make a bad pass, then that gives the riders a straight shot into my goal. My D-men are way out on the wings, my middies are way downfield somewhere, and here comes a fast breaker, all alone.

At least if a pass is bad on the sideline, it either goes out of bounds, which gives us time to get back and set up; or if it's still inbounds, it's way out there and gives my D-men and middies time to get back to the hole. In running straight back toward the goal, at least one or two of them will have a shorter distance to go than an opponent who's just picked up the loose ball way over on the sideline.

But what do you if your only open man is in the middle of the field, say, about 10 yards on the defensive side of the midfield stripe? If the guy is open and is a good 5 yards from any rider, and I know his stickwork is good, and especially if I'm getting pressure from a rider who's about to nail me, or if I'm running out of time to get the ball across midfield, then I'll pass to him. But if he's closely guarded or I still have time, then I'll let him run through his cut and wait for the next one. I try not to force the pass to the middle of the field unless I absolutely have to. To the extent possible, it's best to be patient and work for the highest percentage pass you can get. (Another option is the Gilman, which I'll go over in *Section 10.6* below.) See photo and comments below:

Figure 10-8 – Don't Clear up the Middle…unless…

Comments: In this case (above), the goalie has made the save, his teammates have started to break, and he's waiting for one of them to get farther away from the middle of the field.

However, if one of them – for example, any of the three guys on the far left, is really open (no opponent within 5 or more yards) and has good stickwork, and hopefully good speed, then the goalie can pass to him with some confidence that he can a) catch the ball, and b) move it downfield for the clear.

Note that if none of these three guys gets open, then the goalie will have an outlet pass to the man heading to the right wing.

Figure 10-9 – Be Patient

Comments: Goalie has just made save. A couple guys look open but are a) right in the middle of the field, b) close to the goal, and/or c) still within a step or two of an opponent. Goalie will yell "Break" and wait for one of his teammates to get more open.

10.6 The Gilman

Baltimore's Gilman School has had one of the best high school lacrosse programs for many years. But it's also famous for the Gilman Clear, which basically means heaving the ball downfield as far as you can throw it. If there's absolutely nobody open, depending on the game situation, it's often a good idea.

But note that there's a right and a wrong way to do the Gilman. The goal of the Gilman is to give my guys at least a 50-50 chance of coming up with the ball. To improve the odds, here are some things to keep in mind before you randomly wing the ball downfield:

1) I've had the most success with Gilmans that I throw high and toward one of the far corners, i.e., to the left or right of the goal we're attacking. Throwing a high pass does three things:
    a. A high toss at least gives my attackmen a chance to get down near the ball. If it becomes a footrace between my attackman and his defender, then usually my man will have a good chance of getting there first, since attackers are usually faster than D-men. At worst, they get there at about the same time, and we have a 50-50 chance of coming up with the ground ball.
    b. If you throw a long hard pass with no arc, and nobody can get to it, then it can easily just go out of bounds, especially on a dry field or artificial turf. We lose possession.
    c. If you throw a long hard pass with no arc, and an opponent intercepts it, then they can get the ball back at you quickly and could have an easy fast break.

2) Throwing toward the corner serves two purposes:
    a. First, it keeps the ball out of the middle of the field – as mentioned earlier, clearing up the middle is a bad idea, even on Gilmans. For example, as the goalie winds up to throw that long bomb, he sometimes falls out of his mechanics and ends up tossing a pop-up right to a rider standing near midfield. Again, aim at the far corner, and even if you throw a pop-up, it'll be away from the middle of the field.
    b. Second, when you do get off a long throw, if you've aimed down the middle, the opponent's goalie – who is standing near the crease, unguarded – has a great chance of catching it and sending it right back at you.

3) If you've played or seen golf, the ideal Gilman would be like wedge shot – high so that it won't roll straight out of bounds, and placed so it lands down toward the far corner, about parallel with GLE.
See Figure 10-10 below:

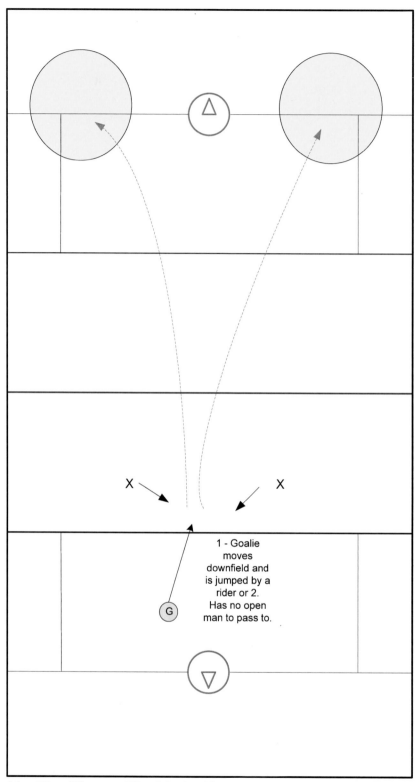

Figure 10-10 – The Gilman: The "dashed" arrows show the pass, which I throw high and aim to land in one of the shaded circles.

I use the Gilman as a last resort, and whenever my clear has completely broken down, and I'm about to get nailed, and I have absolutely no other options. However, before I heave a Gilman, I also take some other factors into consideration:

For example, if there's very little time left in the game, say less than 30 seconds, and we're a goal down, and none of my guys are very open, then I'll probably try to force a pass to a middie or attackman, even if they're guarded fairly closely. If I throw a Gilman in this situation, a lot of time can tick off the clock, and we still have at best a 50-50 chance of getting the ball.

If I force the pass instead, our odds might be only 30-70 or 40-60, but at least we have a chance that my guy will catch the pass and either run in and shoot, or feed to another shooter. With, say, 30 seconds or less to go, this is the best option. It might not work, but at least it gives us a fighting chance. And even if he misses the pass, it might end up on the ground, which is where a Gilman usually ends up anyway. With the ball down, we still could pick it up, and – being in or near the middle of the field – have a better angle on the goal than if I threw a Gilman at a corner.

In the same situation, if the game is tied with only 15 - 25 seconds left, and I have no other options, then I'll throw a Gilman. That gets the ball downfield and gives us a chance at getting another shot. It also eats up some clock, so that even if we don't get the ball or score, the opponent won't have time to get the ball, get it all the way back upfield, and shoot. Then we can take our chances in OT.

The most common Gilman mistakes are implied above, but here's the list:

1) Not throwing the ball far enough.
2) Throwing the ball into the middle of the field.
3) Not throwing the ball high enough.
4) Passing out of bounds near midfield.
5) Waiting too long so that a rider is on top of you before you have a chance to wind up and make a decent long pass.

The Gilman is something you can practice a lot. All you need is another guy to take those long throws. One good set-up is to have your goalies and D-men about 60 yards apart and take turns heaving. Do it both from a standing position and when running.

10.7 Dodging

There is, of course, another option on clears – Goalie as hero, dodging left and right, weaving his way all alone downfield. I'm an ok dodger, but try to avoid it for a couple of reasons.

First, if something goes wrong, like I get checked and lose the ball, then I'm letting down the team by messing around at midfield – this leaves the goal open until I can get back. If a decent team gets the loose ball, they can pass down to the crease in about 2 seconds, which is about 5 seconds faster than I can run back.

Second, I can throw the ball a lot faster than I can run. The objective is to clear the ball within the time limit, so me running around just slows down the process.

Third, the goalie's stick is a really big target. Unless you're really fast and a seasoned dodger, it's fairly easy for a rider to check your stick.

Having said all that, there are times when you'll need to dodge, so I recommend that you learn at least a couple dodges and get good enough to use them if need be. Here are a couple I've used, and there are a lot more. Talk with your middies and attackers, learn a few from them, try a few out and see what suits you best.

In learning to dodge, I've found that it helps to first do the moves slowly, and gradually work up to full speed. See *Section 18.2 - Muscle Memory* for further details.

The descriptions below all assume that you're playing right-handed:

1) **Face Dodge:** Run straight at the defender. Plant your left foot right in front of him, about 3 feet from his feet. As you plant that foot, cradle the ball across your face, then quickly back to the right. As you cradle back to the right, your next step (with your right foot), is to the right. Keep your body between the rider and your stickhead. Run fast.

   One of the great things about the face dodge is that the rider often can't resist poking at your stickhead, just as you're cradling it across your face. But by the time his stick gets to you, you've cradled back across, and his stickhead hits you in the facemask. The ref hears a nice loud "clank," calls the slash, and we get the clear and a man-up situation.

   See Figures 10-11 to 10-14 below:

Figure 10-11 – Face Dodge –
Step 1 – Plant left foot and
begin cradle across face

Figure 10-12 – Face Dodge –
Step 2 – Cradle all the way
across

Figure 10-13 – Face Dodge –
Step 3 – Step w/ right foot and
Bring cradle back to stick-side.

Figure 10-14 – Face Dodge –
Step 4 – Step w/ left foot. Get body
between opponent and stickhead.
Start running & look for a pass.

2) **Circle Dodge:** Run straight at the defender. Plant your left foot right in front of him, about 3 feet from his feet.

As you plant that foot, start to spin clockwise, turning your left side toward the rider, and then your back toward the rider. As you turn, shift over to a left-handed cradle. During all this, keep your body between the rider and your stickhead. Keep turning until you're facing downfield. Pass the ball or run fast.

(Note that this dodge starts off the same way as the face dodge, so you can often throw the rider off by using the face dodge early in the game and then switching to the circle dodge next time – or vice versa.)

Initially, the hardest part of this dodge is the shift over to the left hand. But if you practice enough, and have been working on your left hand, it's not really that difficult.

Figure 10-15 – Circle Dodge,
Step 1
Step in w/ left foot,
Cradle across face

Figure 10-16 – Circle Dodge,
Step 2
Step w/ right foot, toward the right;
bring cradle back to stick-side

Figure 10-17 – Circle Dodge, Step 3
Spinning clockwise, turn back
on opponent. Start switch
to left hand.

Figure 10-18 – Circle Dodge, Step 4
Keep turning clockwise,
Finish switch to left hand

In Steps 3 and 4, keep your body between your stick and the rider.

Figure 10-19 – Circle Dodge, Step 5
Finish the spin, keep running,
look for an open man to pass to.

3) **"Goalie's Swim Move":** OK, it's pretty hard to do a real swim move with a big old goalie stick, but this is as close as I can get. The setup: The rider is coming straight at you, and/or you're running toward him. Or on a dead ball clear, the rider is standing in front of you, and either he starts at you on the whistle, and/or you start at him. Either way, this dodge works best if you're moving straight at each other.

Cock your stick back, just like you do when you're about to pass. Just before you get to him (maybe 5 or 6 feet away), start moving the stickhead forward as if you're passing, but instead of passing, keep your left hand on the butt end of your stick, yank your stick over to the left (the stick handle stays at about 45 degrees), release your right hand, sprint a bit to your left, and turn your right shoulder to the left, so that your body is between the rider and the ball. Switch to your left hand. Run fast.

It seems like this wouldn't fool anybody, but I've seen guys master this move and use it successfully many times in the same game.

Figure 10-20 – Goalie Swim Move - #1: Pretend you're going to pass

Figure 10-21 – Goalie Swim Move - #2: Make it look like a pass is coming...

Figure 10-22 – Goalie Swim
Move - #3:
Bring stick all the way
Across, begin to turn
Counter-clockwise

Figure 10-23 – Goalie Swim
Move - #4:
Continue to turn, drop right
hand off stick, grip butt
end of stick with left hand

Figure 10-24 – Goalie Swim
Move - #5: *Keep turning,*
Switch to left hand

Figure 10-25 – Goalie Swim
Move - #6: *Finish turn*
Keep running and look for pass

10.8 Goalie Takes Off

There are some situations where I'll lead the clear myself by controlling the ball, running down a clear lane, and looking for an open man to pass to.

For example, if a rebound or a loose ball is rolling around in front of the goal, AND if there's nobody else near it, AND if I can get to it before anybody else, AND if I see a clear lane, I'll run out, scoop, and take off downfield, in whatever lane is open (see Figure 10-26 below). This often catches the opponent unaware so that I can get a good 5-yard head start. (Note that I had good footspeed back in the day, and can still run fairly fast for 20 yards or so: But be honest with yourself – if you're a slow runner, you might not want to try this type of clear.)   As I sprint downfield, I look for an open man – ideally to one of my attackmen, who is open in our offensive end, or a middie or D-man breaking downfield parallel to me.

If I have a great jump on the opponent, and know that I can outrun my riders, then I can cross the midfield line and get a fast break started in our end. But if you decide to do this, make sure your pass hits the open man. Some goalies will take the ball across midfield and eventually shoot, but I've never done this because I think the odds are bad in the long run. Yes, I can shoot, and have scored some goals while playing middie and attack.

BUT as a goalie, if I come all the way downfield, shoot and either miss or get saved, then the other team can get the ball going the other way immediately – and there I am, way downfield, 70 yards from my crease. The other team can then get a break going, with just one of my D-men trying to play goalie. Overall, the odds don't favor goalies taking shots, and I don't recommend it. I look for an open man, and pass the ball so that we get the ball downfield as fast as possible, and in the hands of the guys who score goals for a living.

In considering the pros and cons of passing vs. running with the ball, let's look at some numbers:

- If you run 100 yards in 11 seconds (not world-record speed, but not bad), you're going about 18.6 mph, or ~27 feet per second.
- If I throw an average, fairly soft pass, it can easily go 50 mph, or ~ 73 feet per second.
- This means that even a fairly slow pass goes about 3 times as fast as a runner with decent speed.
- QED: In 1 second I can advance the ball 73 feet (by passing) versus only 27 feet (running).

Think about this as you decide whether to run or pass.

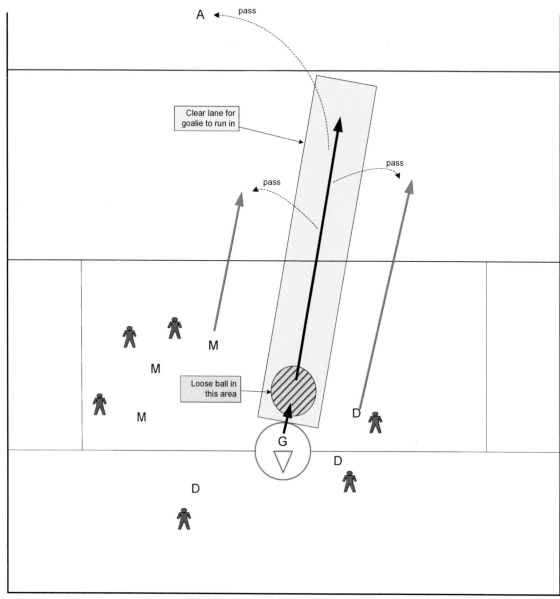

Figure 10-26 – Goalie Takes Off

10.9 Clearing: Summary

Whatever clear you use, note that the goalie has to use a lot of skills: passing, running, dodging, talking to his teammates, knowing what's going on. You need to practice full field clears as much as you can. It's great when your planned clear works, but so many different things can happen and go wrong that a goalie needs to go through hundreds of clears to really be able to make the right split second decisions.

In the off-season or if you can't practice full field, to become better at clearing, the key things to work on are:

1) <u>Seeing the whole field:</u> Practice "sweeping" the whole field with your eyes when you're watching a game.

2) <u>Passing:</u> Especially the touch or lead pass to a guy breaking downfield. And don't forget to practice the Gilman, too: We all need it eventually.

3) <u>Two on ones:</u> With just 3 guys, you can have a good 2-on-1 drill.

4) <u>Dodging:</u> In case you get jumped.

11.0 Conditioning for Goalies: Train for the Game

When I was playing goalie at Princeton, we usually started pre-season practices with a 5-mile run. (As a sprinter and not a distance man, I usually staggered in at the end of the pack…) As we moved into the regular season, this gradually decreased to about a mile before the average practice. This was probably good for the middies, who played both ways in those days, but I'm still not convinced that it helped me become a better goalie: I never actually had to run for five straight miles during a game.

After I left college and started playing club ball, I gradually developed my own approach to conditioning, which is geared toward making a goalie quicker in the cage and faster on his feet. The purpose of this chapter is to share some of my ideas with you.

I'll just tell you what I think has worked fairly well for me, and what hasn't. I'm not a professional fitness expert, and I'm sure there are some things I could or should be doing differently or better. My only testimonial is that at age 58, I played last season with guys much younger than I am – many in their 20's - and had a good year (averaged 4 or 5 goals against, and 10 or 15 saves a game).   At age 55, I played in the Princeton Alumni vs. Varsity game and during my 15 minutes in the cage, the Varsity didn't score on me, and I made saves against guys like Ryan Boyle and Jason Doneger. In the Fall 2007 game (at age 58), I played a quarter against the Varsity and let in only one goal. This isn't to say that I'm the greatest goalie in the world, by any means, but it shows that I can still compete with the youngsters. And I think it's some evidence that my training program has helped me to stay competitive, even at my advanced age. Likewise, I think it will help young goalies to get in shape for what really happens in games – making saves, throwing accurate passes, sprinting on clears, and staying focused for all four quarters.

11.1 General Fitness

From a fitness point of view, my main objectives are to stay fairly healthy, and do whatever it takes to be the best goalie I can be. Enough has been written and taught about general fitness so that I don't have to repeat all that. In summary:

- Eat a healthy, well-balanced diet, low on sugars and saturated fats.
- Get plenty of sleep. Tests have shown that reflexes slow down if you're tired – this seems obvious, but is worth repeating.
- It goes without saying that you should avoid alcohol, cigarettes and other types of stimulants, depressants and even many over-the-counter drugs. All these things will tend to slow you down and/or make you inconsistent in the cage.

11.2 Goalie Objectives

But this article is about playing goalie in lacrosse, so what do I do to get ready for the season? What do I do during the season? What has worked and what hasn't helped much?

First, I want to back up and state explicitly exactly what my objectives are as a goalie:

1) Make my reflexes as fast as possible.

2) Be able to run fairly fast during clears and loose balls.

3) Have enough strength to throw a hard or a long pass when I have to.

4) Have enough physical and mental endurance to be able to focus intensely during the whole game.

5) Be solid enough to take the physical abuse I get when playing goalie.

I'll look at each of these in turn, but first a note: For me, 90% of staying in shape is showing up every day and working as hard as I can at whatever exercise I'm doing. I don't do anything fancy, but I do it every day.

Objective #1: Make my reflexes as fast as possible.

There are two main types of muscle used for moving around: Slow twitch and fast twitch. There are a lot of scientific studies about these types of muscle, which you might find interesting. You can look this up on the Web or in a library, so I'll just give the basics: Slow twitch muscle fiber contracts more slowly, but has more long-term endurance than fast twitch, which is basically the opposite: Less endurance, but capable of a faster rate of contraction.

In the average person, most muscles (like your bicep, for instance) are about half slow twitch and half fast. It appears that people are born with a genetically predetermined percentage of slow and fast twitch muscle. Percentages vary, and having a lot of one or the other can help you in certain sports. For example:

> "Olympic sprinters have been shown to possess about 80% fast twitch fibers, while those who excel in the marathon may have 80% slow twitch fibers."
> (From Fast and Slow Twitch Muscle Fibers, by Elizabeth Quinn, http://sportsmedicine.about.com/cs/exercisephysiology/a/aa080901a.htm)

From what I've read, there has been no scientific proof that an individual can significantly change the percentage of slow and fast switch muscle that he's born with.

However, with conditioning, a person can improve the performance of what he has. For example, by running distances and similar exercises, you can make your slow twitch muscles more efficient. Likewise, by doing certain exercises, you can help your fast twitch muscles to fire faster.

As a goalie, this is what I want: Fast twitch muscles that "GO" when I need to make a save. If you take a quick look at the web, and do a search on "fast twitch muscle," you'll see thousands of results (I got 191,000). Some websites and companies claim that if you drink, eat or rub on their product, your fast twitch muscles will work better. I can't speak to all these claims – I can only tell you what I do. The fact that I can still make some tough saves at age 58 should mean that I'm doing something right. Maybe I could do better, but here's my simple approach.

Diet: First, I don't take any special pills, powders or supplements, and I don't recommend them. Think of your motto as "I'm not on steroids, but thanks for asking." You get in shape by working hard, not by taking pills. I just eat a balanced diet and try to keep the sweets and fats fairly low. I'm not overly thin and not fat.

Lifting: Lifting weights in a certain way has been an effective way to keep my fast twitch muscles good shape. During the off-season, I lift twice a week and just go through a fairly standard set of upper body and leg exercises: curls, bench press, etc. Any decent gym or fitness expert can give you a good, well-balanced weight program that addresses your major muscle groups. I'm not lifting to make really giant muscles: If a goalie gets too "big," I think it will reduce flexibility and slow him down.

Before lifting, it's good to loosen up by walking or running for 10 minutes or so, and by doing some light stretching. This improves the flow of synovial fluid in the joints, which helps to lubricate and cushion cartilage and other tissues.

Everything I've read and everybody I've talked to says that you should inhale on the "easy" part of the lift and exhale when contracting the muscle you're working. For example, when doing a bicep curl, you inhale as you extend the arm straight down, and then exhale as you curl/contract the bicep.

When I contract a muscle in a lift (e.g., a curl), I do it really fast in a single burst, because when I make a save move, I'm going do have to contract various muscles in an instant. Try this with light weights first, because you don't want to strain a tendon, ligament or muscle on Day 1. In summary, when I contract the muscle during the lift, I don't make a long, lazy contraction; instead, I "pop" the contraction as fast as I can.

Another point: On both parts of the lift, make sure you contract all the way (e.g., curl the weight all the way up), and then extend all the way down. This ensures that the muscle, ligaments and tendons get full extension in both directions. Lifters who "short-arm" their lifts end up with less flexible tissues that can tear more easily when stressed in a game.

I usually do three sets of each exercise (curl, fly, etc.), starting with a light weight that I can do 25 or 30 times, and gradually work my way up to a weight where I can only do 12 or 15 reps. When I feel like I'm getting a little too stiff or bulky, I back down to lighter weights.

After a session, which usually takes me about an hour and a half, it's good to stretch all the muscles you used and keep them warm by putting on sweats.

During the season, I don't lift any less than 3 days before a game. Maybe this is my age, but I feel like my body needs those 3 days to recover from a session.

So far, this approach has worked pretty well for me. Warming up ahead of time and not lifting really heavy weights has prevented pulls and strains. And overall, I think that lifting on a regular basis helps to keep the fast twitch muscles ready to fire quickly. Remember: For goalies, the objective isn't to have the best bod on the beach – it's to finely hone your fast twitch muscles so that they'll fire really fast when you need to make a save.

Hand and Foot Speed: Lifting will help keep your fast twitch muscles ready to go, but there are a few other things that can improve your hand and foot speed.

Hand Speed: I've found that any activity requiring quick hands and hand/eye coordination helps to improve hand speed. After college I worked as a waterman on the Chesapeake Bay. Without going into the wet, muddy details, I'll just say that oystering and handling fish net required quick hands, all day long. During club ball in the summer, I found that this work translated into much faster hand speed than I had had before.

I'm not recommending that all goalies should grab a set of oyster tongs, but here are a few activities that can help: Ping pong, air hockey, playing drums, racquet sports, martial arts, boxing, and anything else you can think of.

Foot Speed: In my experience, a lot of goalies and coaches focus less on foot speed and more on hand speed, i.e., moving the stick to the shot as fast as possible. Quick hands are obviously key to making saves, but in my mind, the best goalies are often those who have not only speedy hands, but remarkably fast feet. Here's how quick feet help:

- Taking that first fast step "leads" all the rest of the mechanics that follow in a great save move. Muscle memory for making a complete save move includes a full sequence of motions. By initiating this sequence with a really fast first step, the rest of the movements will follow more quickly than if your first step is slow.
- The first step gets the lead foot in line with the shot. On really fast shots, sometimes the foot is all that can get there in time. For example, on an offside low shot, the lead foot has to move only, say, 18 inches, while the stickhead has to travel up to about 48 inches.

171

There are lots of drills that can improve footspeed.

- My favorite is to get in the ready-to-save stance and just practice stepping to the ball. I start off slowly and gradually work up to full speed. I make it a contest with myself to see how fast I can go. This not only improves footspeed, but also "burns in" muscle memory at maximum speed. I vary the drill by stepping to imaginary stick-side and offside low, hip-high and high shots. Doing this for 15 minutes a day can really improve footspeed and improve the muscle memory you need to make save moves.
- Jumping rope is great for footspeed. You can practice lots of different types of steps as you jump.
- Stand at the foot of the stairs. Step up with your left foot, then up with your right, down with your left, down with you right. Repeat for as long and as fast as you can.
- Play other sports: Basketball, football, soccer, volleyball, and many other sports require quick feet and bursty speed.

Objective #2: Be able to run fairly fast during clears and loose balls.
So…how does a goalie get to be a fast runner? Frankly, some people are just faster sprinters than others. All other things being equal, a key factor is the amount of fast twitch muscle you have and how well trained that muscle is. To get faster, you need to get the most out of whatever fast twitch you have, and the weight training described in Item 1 above can help.

But just lifting isn't enough – you have to run! For goalies, I recommend lots of wind sprints. This approach emulates what happens in a game:

a. A shot goes wide and I sprint 10 yards to the OOB line.
b. There's a loose ball out front - I have a chance to get to it first, dash out, scoop, run 15 yards and pass to an open man.
c. On a dead ball clear, a rider comes after me and I have to dodge, run away from him, and keep going or throw a pass.

In all of these cases, I seldom run more than 20 or 30 yards at a time. The key is to be as fast as I can for those 20-30 yards, and get right back to the cage after I pass the ball. I then have to recover quickly and be ready to make a save and run again. Wind sprints are the best drill I've found to get me in shape for all this.

When I start running sprints, I just go 10 yards up, fairly slowly, 10 yards back. Take a breather. Then 20 yards, and so on, up to 50. Gradually I work up to faster and faster speeds, until I'm doing an all-out sprint. Before the season I usually run wind sprints every other day. This gives my legs a chance to recover during the off-day. Once the season starts, I cut back (depending on how many games I have during a week). I usually run a lot during games, and at my age, it takes a couple of days for my legs to recover, so I don't overdo it.

Here are a couple of technical things that seem to help me run a little faster. First, when starting to run from a standing position, I get as low as I can, gradually raising up as I accelerate. When I reach full speed, it helps to stay fairly straight up. If running without a stick, you can go faster if you keep your arms close to your sides, pumping hard. But the stick makes this a little tough. In general, I try to use this "sprinter form" when I'm running wind sprints, but also run with a stick and cradle a ball, to get used to the adjustments I have to make for handling the ball, passing, getting in good position to take a pass, and so on.

There are "speed coaches" who know a lot more than I do. You or your coach might want to check one out and see what they have to offer.

Objective #3: Have enough strength to throw a hard pass when I have to.
Lifting weights will help with this, but also just practicing your passing. At the beginning of every practice, and before every game, after some stretching, walking and jogging, I always throw some passes. I start with short passes, and gradually work my way up to longer distances. Tossing the ball around not only gets me ready for the passing I'll do in the game, but seems to "warm my eyes up," as I focus on watching the ball closely. This gets me geared up for the warm-up in the cage, which comes right after the passing.

The key to good passing is using good form, as passing isn't just brute force. Strength helps, but the length of the "arc" when throwing is a main factor in determining distance. By that I mean, for example, if you slide your top hand up near the stickhead, the ball won't go that far. But if you have your bottom hand down near the butt end on the stick, and the top hand only, say 16 or 18 inches above the butt, and if you keep your arms away from your body, then you develop a long arc when you throw and you'll get a lot more distance on your passes.

In any case, having good arm strength will help you throw more accurately and farther. Arm strength will also help you to throw a real bullet, though note that most passes should have some "air under them," as the laser-rockets are harder to catch. Having strong arms will help you to control the speed, distance, arc and touch you put on the ball.

Objective #4: Have enough physical and mental endurance to be able to focus intensely during the whole game.
Here comes the fun part…Playing goalie doesn't look all that strenuous, and it's not, at least from a long distance running point of view. However, the goalie has to keep up a high level of mental intensity for the whole game. I've found that I have to have lots of physical stamina to keep up that full game's worth of high intensity mental focus. Your brain and mind burn an incredible number of calories, especially if you're paying as much attention as a goalie needs to pay.

Also, being in the "ready to save" stance for several minutes at a time can wear out your legs, especially the thighs. For me, doing 10 or 15 minutes on the Stairmaster or similar machine has really helped. Weight training for the legs is also good. Leg presses, squats, wall slides, leg curls, toe raises, knee 'extensions' and similar exercises will all help to build up your legs. I work these into my lifting a couple times a week.

I've even heard goalies complain that their arms can get tired by the 4th quarter. And I've seen goalies whose arm action looks a little slower toward the end of a game. You wouldn't think that a lacrosse stick can get heavy, but the main point is that your arms need to be able to make save moves really fast throughout the whole game – just as fast in the last minute of the game as in the first. Lifting weights in the ways described above will help with this problem, but general endurance training will help not only your legs, but also your arms. I use one of those machines for "pedaling with your arms," which really helps in a way that straight lifting can't.

There are lots of ways to build physical stamina: Running, elliptical, bike, stairs, etc. I prefer the elliptical, bike and stairs because they don't cause high impact stress to my legs. Young people's legs can hold up better than mine, so running a mile every other day is a great way to build endurance, and doesn't require any special equipment. But hopefully your coach or trainer will know that even youngsters can get shin splints and similar injuries, and won't pound you too hard. If you have a choice, I recommend running on grass, not pavement, which is hard on the legs, especially over an extended period of time.

Objective #5: Be solid enough to take the physical abuse I get when playing goalie

All the running, biking, cardio, stretching and lifting help to make a goalie "solid" all over. A goalie needs to absorb the pounding of getting hit by shots, knocked down, run into and all the general rough-and-tumble of a typical lacrosse game.

For example, I've found that when I'm in shape and have been following my conditioning program, getting hit in the thigh or forearm with a shot will leave a bruise but not really hurt much during or after a game. When playing club ball many years ago, I didn't work out much between games - and the bruises and muscle tweaks hurt more and lasted longer. When I hit my 30's, I started working out a lot more and have seldom had any nagging problems.

11.3 Other Sports and Activities

As lacrosse gets more popular, I've noticed that a lot of players are dropping out of other sports and spending all their time with a stick in their hand. I guess this might make them better, just because they spend more time passing, shooting and dodging. On the other hand, I think there's a serious risk of burn-out, especially if a kid starts playing "full-time" when he's only 10 or even 8. The fact is that you can get sick of even a great sport like lacrosse.

Personally, I think kids should play other sports if they enjoy them and want to play. First, other sports are fun and can offer the same benefits as lacrosse – learning sportsmanship, being part of a team, working hard to improve. Second, it helps prevent lacrosse burnout. Third, a player will pick up skills in other sports that are really useful in lacrosse. For example, in my case, I think my feet got a bit quicker from playing soccer. In baseball, as an infielder, I learned how to get down on a ball and had to be quick with my hands. When batting, I learned how to pick up a fastball coming out pitcher's hand – very similar to picking up a shot coming out of a stick. Wrestling required lots of conditioning and strength, not to mention intense focus, quick reflexes and mental toughness. I think that playing these sports helped make me a better lacrosse goalie.

Other sports can also help out. Football offers the same type of contact and bursty play that you see in lacrosse. The offensive and defensive plays in basketball are very similar to what's done in lacrosse. Cross country and crew require lots of endurance and training discipline. Tennis, ping-pong and racquetball hone reflexes. I helped coach one high school goalie who had been doing martial arts for several years. I don't know much about Karate or Tae Kwon Do, but this kid had great reflexes, strength, concentration and endurance.

In summary, other sports don't hurt your lacrosse game and will usually help it out. But I can see focusing only on lacrosse if you're a senior in high school and are good enough to shoot for a college scholarship. In that case, it might make sense to work on your conditioning and lacrosse skills all fall and winter, rather than be a sub on the football team.

11.4 Choices

All this talk of conditioning and other sports makes for a busy day. Plus we all have school, jobs, friends, socializing and important TV shows to watch. I find myself thinking: How am I going to fit all this in?

The answer isn't always easy. Sure, it would be great to make a living just playing ball. But frankly, even many of the best players in the world – the guys in the MLL and NLL – don't make enough on playing lacrosse alone, and I suspect that most of them have other jobs.

Having said that, if you love playing lacrosse, and want to become the best player possible, then you need to make time to get in shape, practice and play a lot. For me, this has meant that I've had to make choices:

- Do I go to the gym or sit on my rear end watching TV?
- Do I go play some wall ball or ride around town with my buddies?
- Do I practice my stance and my stepping or read a video game magazine?

The choice is yours. I'm not saying that you have to live and breathe lacrosse 24/7, but the fact is you won't get better unless you practice and get in shape. Each person will find his own balance between Lacrosse and Everything Else.

In my case, a long time ago, I cut back on some things like watching TV and generally goofing off to spend more time working out and practicing. I got better, and the trade-off has been worth it to me.

For what it's worth, during the off-season, my conditioning program is something like this:

- <u>Day 1:</u> Hard Cardio/endurance work. 90 minutes. Legs (running, bike, stairs, elliptical) and arms (arm pedaling machine).
- <u>Day 2:</u> Light cardio for 45 minutes.
- <u>Day 3:</u> Upper body and leg weight training. 90 minutes.
- <u>Repeat:</u> Over and over.

Also, I started doing some simple yoga stretches almost 30 years ago when I had a back injury. I'm not into the "spiritual" side of it, but I still do it every morning for 20 – 30 minutes. I think it helps keep the muscles, ligaments and tendons stretched and flexible, and I've had only a few minor problems since I started with it.

Overall, in high school I spent about 2 to 2.5 hours a day playing lacrosse or some other sport. In college, in the fall I played soccer (2 to 2.5 hours a day); in the winter I worked out or practiced lacrosse (2 hours a day); and during the season, practice and conditioning took about 3 hours a day.

In the past few years of playing club ball, I spend about 1 to 2 hours a day either exercising, practicing lacrosse, or playing in a game. This is what's worked for me, but you'll need to find out what suits you. If you have trouble figuring out what program is producing the best results, start writing down what exercises you do every day, and also how well you played that day and subsequent days. You may find some correlations, e.g., you're slower the day after you lift. If this happens, you might want to decrease the amount of weight and the number of reps, or move your workout day.

Goalie is a tough position – both physically and mentally. But by getting in shape and "training for the game," as I've outlined above, you'll give yourself the best possible shot at honing those fast twitch muscles for making saves, running fast, and having enough endurance to focus intensely for every minute of every game. No matter what conditioning program you choose, do it every day and you'll see results on the field. As I said, 90 percent of getting in shape is showing up and working hard every day.

12.0 Man-down

Now that you're in great shape, let's get back to the field. Goalies ask me a lot: What do I do when we're a man down? In summary, the goalie doesn't really do much that's different from all-even play. The stance, positioning, watching the ball, etc. all remain the same.

12.1 Man Down – Basic Set-ups

Figures 12-1 and 12-2 show typical man-down offensive sets. The Green guys are the offense (A through F), while the X's represent the defense. When you're man down, you want the opponent to have to shoot from outside the shaded semi-circle. The usual plan is that the goalie saves anything cranked from outside this range, while the defense keeps anybody from cutting inside, taking a feed, and shooting from only a few feet out.

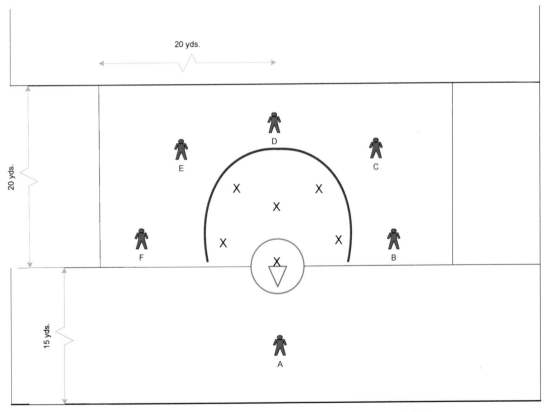

Figure 12-1: Man Down – Offense in "Perimeter" Set-up

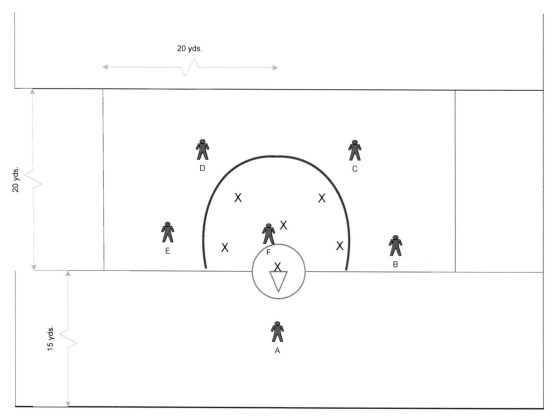

Figure 12-2: Man Down – Attackman on Crease

I don't want to tell your coach how to play against these and other offensive sets. I just want to point out a few things that the goalie needs to focus on, regardless of what defensive package your coach decides to use.

12.2 What's Different for the Goalie?

The first difference is that the goalie has to make sure that all his teammates a) know that you're a man down, and b) know what defense to get into.

<u>Talk – What to watch for and what to yell</u>
When a penalty is first called, and your man goes into the box, it's obvious that you need to go into your man-down defense. However, believe it or not, sometimes a guy on the sideline won't be paying much attention, will suddenly hear his name called to "Get in the game," and he runs on, not realizing that you have to be in man-down D. Or he wasn't paying attention in practice that week, and doesn't know what position to play when he gets in.

So...the goalie's job is to make sure everybody knows what's going on. He has to yell something like "OK, we're man-down. Get into Blue defense," or whatever scheme you're using for man-down. He also has to make sure each defender knows where to set up.

To reiterate: The goalie has to really take over and run the defense, especially calling out "Who's hot?" or "Ed, you're hot," and calling the slides that go with the defensive package. You should be doing this when you're all even too, but it's especially important to keep your D on their toes during man-down.

<u>When the penalty is up</u>
Once the penalty is over and your man comes back on the field, don't yell "All even" until the guy is actually back into position to play defense, and is guarding somebody. I've seen lots of goalies – and players on the bench – yell "All even" the second the guy steps from the box onto the field. The D then relaxes a little, goes out of the man-down D, and the opponent gets a quick goal.

Once the guy is back playing D, then the goalie's job is to let everybody know. Say something like "All even. Get back into Green. Get your man. Who's got number 5?," and so on.

<u>Loose Ball</u>
If the man-up offense loses the ball, the defense sometimes has a tendency to <u>all</u> run out after it. Everything I said about this in *Section 9.6* still holds true, except that the goalie has to really make sure his D-men don't go too far out. If the opponent quickly recovers and gets the ground ball, and two of your D-men are out past the restraining line, all it takes is one fast pass to put the offense into a 5 on 3. Talk to your defense and tell them where to go. They often lose track of how far out they are, so tell them when to get back.

12.3 Typical Plays to Watch out for

As goalie, here are the main things to watch out for when you're man down. Most opponents will have a favorite play, where they're trying to set up an open shooter. Most man-down goals come from rockets from a completely open middie shooting from 6 to 10 yards, screens, cuts to open space on the crease, and back door cuts – and most teams will favor one or two of these. You'll have to know this from a scouting report, or just by watching how they pass the ball and cut.

For example, if they work the ball around fast and try to feed the open middie at right front, before your defense can slide back to him, then the goalie has to be really fast at getting into the right spot on the arc and into the "ready to save" stance. This tests your ability to be in the right position and move on the arc quickly – all things I've talked about in previous sections of this book. Again, you should be doing this anyway, but when you're a man down, there is even less time than usual for any delay, even a split second.

Or if the opponent is trying to sneak a guy around to the back door, you have to let your D-man on that corner know that, so he can possibly cheat a little and be ready to cut off the passing lane and/or hit the guy coming around. Meanwhile, the goalie has to be ready to go from pipe to pipe really fast. If the ball is at right front, and the cutter is sneaking around to the Left Pipe crease, then you'll need to get to the Left Pipe asap. Like everything else, this takes practice.

12.4 Planning Ahead, then Executing the Plan

A lot of man-down goals are scored simply because everybody on the defense doesn't know what package they're in, where they're supposed to set up, and where and when they're supposed to slide. All it takes is one clueless D-man to cost your team 3 or 4 goals a game, which is often the difference between winning and losing.

Your coach will have some man-down drills, and should have a pre-set group of guys who go in whenever there's a penalty. If one of these guys committed the foul, then – before the game - the coach needs to choose another guy to go in – and this guy needs to immediately know where to go, what the package is, and everything else about the set-up you're in. As goalie, I recommend that you take the man-down drills seriously:

1) First, make sure you <u>know and do what you're supposed to be doing</u> (e.g., getting to the right place on the arc as the passes whiz around).

2) Second, as goalie, you <u>need to know exactly what every other D-man is supposed to be doing</u>. If a guy is out of position or not sliding to the right place, at the right time, then you need to tell him what to do – loud and fast. In short, the goalie needs to learn "the whole playbook," so it's best to pay attention when the coach is walking through all the slides in practice.

With a well-planned, well-organized man-down D, you can prevent goals most of the time. As goalie, one of your jobs is to make sure everybody understands that, knows what to do, and does it.

13.0 Fast Breaks

Fast breaks are similar to man-down, in that the offense has one more guy than you do. The difference is obviously that the break often happens before the D can get into a package. If the break happens off a face-off or on a quick clear, then you should already have a play set up to deal with it. Before the face-off, I always tell my three D-men which one has the point on the break – which is always the guy in the middle.

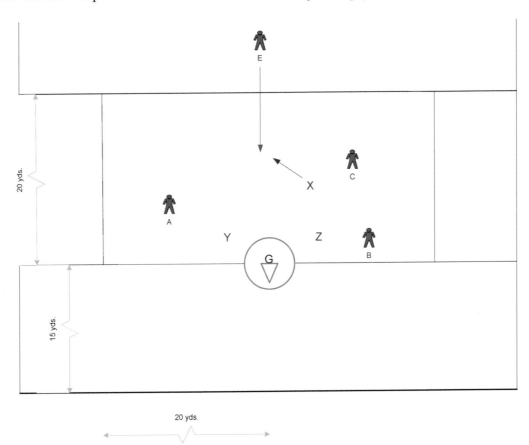

20 yds.

15 yds.

20 yds.

Figure 13-1: Typical Fast Break off a Face-off or Quick Clear

Comment: Opponent E has the ball on the break. Our D-man – X – has the point, and has to go after E when E is, say, 12 to 15 yards from the goal. If X goes too soon, then he gives E an easy pass – probably to C – and also takes himself out of the rest of the play by being too far from the goal.

But if X goes too late, and nobody else picks up E, then E just runs in unguarded and shoots for what should be an easy goal.

After X makes his move out to cover E, then your coach's slide packages will kick into action.

No matter what these packages are, on fast breaks, the goalie will have to be able to move quickly, and get to the right spot on the arc in an instant. If the attack works the break properly, they'll "whipsaw" the goalie by drawing him to one side of the cage, and then passing across the field to an open man on the other side of the crease. Therefore, to deal with fast breaks, the goalie needs to be able to go from one pipe to the other in less time than it takes for a feed to get across to a cutter. See Figure 13-2 below for a depiction of what often happens.

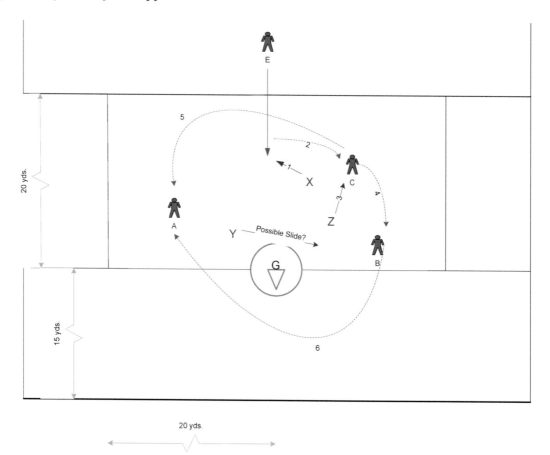

Figure 13-2 – Fast Break – Typical Sequence of Passes and Slides

Comments:
1) D-man X goes out to guard Attacker E.
2) E passes to C
   (C shoots if D-man Z doesn't guard him.)
3) If D-man Z goes out to guard C, then C passes to the open man, which will be:
4) to Attacker B – if Y doesn't slide to the right to cover B, or
5) to Attacker A if Y *does* slide to the right.
6) If Y slides to the right and B gets the pass, then that leaves A open at Left Top, for a feed from B.

As you follow this sequence of passes and slides, you'll see that the ball might well go to Attackman B, who is at Right Pipe. In this case, the goalie goes to the "Right Pipe" position on the arc and gets ready for a shot. But if Attackman B then passes across to Attackman A, who is at Left Top, then the goalie has to immediately get over to the other side of the arc, ready for a shot from Left Front.

Your coach will have set up what the D needs to do on this type of break, and hopefully you'll have practiced this countless times. If you are playing club ball and never practice (like me), then before the game, I always go over who does what on a break. And when I see a break coming down, I always get ready to move really quickly on the arc.

Other breaks – off unsettled situations – are harder to deal with than the face-off break. The unsettled break can come from anywhere, any time, but usually when a few guys are fighting for a loose ball outside, the offense picks it up and gets off a quick feed. In this case, the goalie yells out "Break" and starts telling his defenders what to do. In these situations, one typical problem is that nobody goes after the guy with the ball, call him #10. The guy who normally guards #10 has been off chasing the loose ball. The other D-men know that they haven't been guarding #10, so they hang back and guard somebody else. #10 sprints in untouched and fires in a goal from 8 feet.

In this case, the goalie has to tell a specific D-man to go get #10, and also tell everybody else to get ready to slide. This all happens in a split second, but good defenses do it all the time. Like everything else, it takes practice, and I hope your coach has a drill for the "fast break off a loose ball."

14.0 One-on-Ones

The question I get from goalies more than any other is "How do I deal with 1-on-1's?" If I had a fool-proof answer to this, I'd probably be starting on the US National Team. In fact, there's no easy answer. 1-on-1's are arguably the hardest type of shot to stop: The harsh truth is that a decent shooter should be able to score every time when he's on the crease, alone with the goalie, or running in unguarded.

So what's a goalie supposed to do? The answers are similar to what I wrote about in *Section 6.0* (above). To review, here's what I said (slightly modified to cover all 1-on-1's, not just an attacker coming from behind):

- You'll have to make the crucial judgment call: Do I go out or stay back? In general, if you're playing against shooters with decent talent, it's a mistake to go out. Once you commit, they know where you are, and will just shoot at whatever part of the goal isn't covered. The other thing to look for is: "Is the shooter cocked and ready to shoot?" If he's just finished a tough dodge and just bulled past your D-man...and if his stick isn't yet in a position he can shoot from, AND if he's close enough for you to reach him, then by all means, take a fast step or two out and lay into him before he can lock and load. When you decide to do this, go hard. Don't just wave your stickhead at him or his stick - go out stick-on-stick, lower your shoulder, and nail him in the middle of his body.

  I don't mean for you to try to hurt him – there's no place for cheap shots in lacrosse – but hey, it's a contact sport, and if a guy gets too close to your crease, it's often a good idea to give him a nice clean hit. I recommend practicing this – Have guys come [at you 1-on-1] and learn how to step out and nail them. It doesn't have to be a bloodbath, but you need to try it a lot before game-time. It's good for you and your attackmen.

- <u>When to stay back</u>: BUT, if the shooter dodged the D-man somewhere back near X and has had time to get his stick ready to shoot, and isn't coming within 3 or so feet of the crease as he comes around, then I recommend holding your ground...and getting in your best "ready to save" stance. Hopefully, a slide will come in a second, but if it doesn't, all you can do is improve your odds. Here are a couple things to try in this situation:

- <u>Watching his stick position</u>: When a guy comes [in] unguarded, his stick will be in one of three general areas: high, hip-height or low.

1) <u>Stickhead High:</u> If his stickhead is high, I keep in my normal stance but make sure that my stickhead stays high.

   o *High shot:* If he shoots high, at least I have a chance at it. If he shoots low, then I might not have time to get the stickhead down, but I rely on my feet and legs – more on the feet in *Section 7.0 – Stepping to the Ball, and Section 20.1 - My Unorthodox Technique on Low Shots.*

   o *Low Shot:* See Figure 6-45 above: This picture shows a shot where I can't get my stick down in time, but have "snapped" my legs together to make the low save with my foot, shin, knee or thigh.

   o *Waist Level Shot:* If the shot comes at me at waist level, I might not be able to get my stick down in time, and my feet and shins won't do any good, but I've often been able to use my legs to drive my thigh or one side of my midsection into the path of the shot.

2) <u>Stickhead Hip-High:</u> Guys sometimes come [in] with the stickhead at hip height. In this case, I use pretty much the same approach as when his stickhead is high: I keep my stickhead high for the high shots, feet and legs ready for a low ball, and midsection or thigh for in between.

3) <u>Stickhead Low:</u> One thing I've seen a lot is guys breaking free from a D-man, [speeding across the face of the goal], and trying to whip in a low sidearm shot. (Sometimes they even dive and shoot as they get near the ground.) This is the one case where I'll drop my stick down and "get big" down low. If the distance between his stickhead and me is only a few feet, then getting my big crosse in the way cuts down the angle with a lot more surface area than my legs. I stay in the "ready to save" stance, but have my stickhead right down next to my left calf (remember, I'm left-handed). Even if he's able to get off a shot that's heading high, my cutting off the angle often snuffs this shot before it goes too far. And, as always, if I miss the low shot with my stick, I'm ready to snap my legs together to make a foot or leg save.

To summarize, and make general statements about any 1-on-1, whether the guy is coming around the corner or from out front:

It's usually a bad idea to rush out and try to hit his stick, especially if he's more than a yard away from you. If he has good control of the ball, once you start out, you're committing yourself, and he'll easily shoot past you. For example, if he's any good, he can easily fake high – then if you go high for the fake, and start into a "high save move," he can just drop down and shoot low.

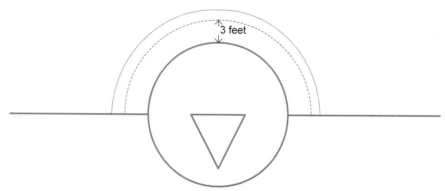

Figure 14-1 – When to go out

Comments: The distance from the crease to the "dashed" line is about 3 feet. From the crease to the dotted line is about 5 feet.

If an opponent is between the "3-foot" line and the crease, and is about to take a feed, the goalie might have a good chance of getting to him before he can catch the feed, control it and shoot. But nothing is etched in stone, and the goalie's decision – whether to go out after him and try to either stuff the shot or hit his stick – will depend on a number of factors:

    1) <u>How close is the goalie standing to the guy?</u>

        a. For example, if you're out on a high arc and see a feed coming to a potential feeder who is planted within the blue circle, then you probably have a good chance of getting to him just as the pass arrives, or slightly after arrival.

        b. But if the ball is at Right Back or X, and you're only, say, 18 inches off the goal line, when you turn to face the potential feeder, you're 8 or 10 feet from the shooter. It'll take at least 2 steps and a long time to move 8 or 10 feet for a stuff. In this case, you're better off hanging back, getting into your ready-to-save stance, and not committing before he shoots.

        c. If the potential shooter is between 3 and 5 feet out from the crease, then getting out in time for the stuff is hard, even if you're on a high arc and are fairly quick at this move.

        d. If the shooter is more than 5 feet out, then in my experience, it's extremely difficult to get out to him in time for a stuff – unless the feed is coming slowly and/or on a high arc. In this case, it's better to stay back, get in a good position and react to the shot as fast as you can.

    2) <u>How fast is the goalie at getting out to people?</u> You have to know your own skills. Practice this play a lot to see if you're quick enough to get there in time. If not, stay back, get in a good ready-to-save stance, watch the ball, and get ready to make a save move.

186

3) *How fast is the feed traveling?* *If it's a bullet, then it's often all I can do to turn around and get into a ready-to-save stance. In these cases, I don't even think about going for the stuff, unless I'm within a couple feet of the shooter. But if it's a lob onto a guy standing on or near the crease, and I judge that I can get to the shooter before the ball does, or just as the ball arrives, then I'll go out and try to stuff him or at least check his stick and give him a solid body check.*

I usually go for a straight hard poke to the shaft - <u>unless</u> he's just about to catch the feed or has just caught it. Catching means he has to freeze the stickhead in one spot for at least an instant, and that's when I'll go for his mesh with my stickhead – IF I can get my stickhead to his stickhead in time. If I'm late with this move, then I'll have committed high and be vulnerable to a guy who catches the feed, sees my stickhead high, and drops down just a bit to shoot right past me.

So, on a 1-on-1, unless I can nail his stickhead, I don't go out, but just stay in my best "ready to save" stance and get ready to react. See Figures 14-2 through 14-4 below.

One thing I should mention: I've found that it's best to "clear off the crease" early in the game. What I mean by this is that the first time there's a feed to a guy on the crease, I'll make sure I'm aggressive in going out, whacking his stick, and giving him a nice, solid body check. If the goalie and his D-men let the opponents run free, untouched near the crease early in the game, then this gives them confidence and makes them think they can get in close whenever they want.

Obviously, you don't want this to happen, so I like to set the tone as early in the game as possible. I want to send a message: "This is <u>my</u> crease. If you come around here, you're going to get nailed." When I do this effectively in the first quarter, it can take away a big piece of their offense. They then have to try other ways to score, hopefully something they're not as good at.

Figure 14-2 – One on One: Goalie stays in position

Comment: One thing I like about this situation is that the goalie has stayed in a solid "ready to save" stance and stayed in the right spot on the arc. Plus he's kept his stickhead at the same height as the shooter's.

Figure 14-3 – One on One: Goalie stayed in position and made a great save.

Remember that even the best players make mistakes and will sometimes hit a goalie with a shot. As you go down the scale in skill levels, more and more shooters aren't perfect and there's at least a decent chance of them hitting you or even missing the goal – IF you're in a good stance and the right position. Sticking to these fundamentals gives you a better chance than if you go out on him and commit too early.

By the way, there's some pressure on the shooter too. He might be just an average player who happened to come up with a ground ball and get a clear lane to the goal. Maybe he doesn't even shoot very often. He's probably thinking, "Oh my gosh, this should be so easy, if I miss it I'll look so stupid." If he sees you standing there cool and confident, it'll worry him even more, and hopefully he'll tighten up. And when guys tighten up, then usually don't take good shots.

Above all, don't panic. The 1-on-1 is a real test of whether you're able to keep your cool and stick with your fundamentals and solid mechanics: Get and stay in a good stance, watch the ball intensely, and make a proper save move when he shoots. Step to the ball and get your stick there as fast as you can, just as you would on any shot from, say, 15 yards.

Don't think that something unusual like jumping up, going to your knees, or waving your stick around will help. If you start to freak out, it's more likely that you'll forget the basic good save moves and do something uncoordinated and unsuccessful. Yes, you occasionally see a goalie jump and make a save, but for every time this works, there are 10 times that it doesn't. If you jump, you're just giving the guy the entire lower part of the goal. Likewise, if you go to your knees, you give him the whole top half of the net.

Figure 14-4 – One on One: hang in there - Don't panic, don't jump, don't guess

Guessing?

This leads me to another age-old question I hear a lot: Should a goalie guess where the attacker will shoot? I don't believe in guessing and never do it. I'd rather wait til I see the shot, and then rely on good fundamentals and my reflexes. It's true that some goalies who guess occasionally make a save. But even more often, they guess wrong and the ball hits the back of the net.

Figure 14-5 – Guessing Wrong

Comment: The Yellow goalie (partially obscured) guessed that the Red Jersey (far right) would shoot low and to the goalie's right. You can see that the goalie has stepped and moved his stickhead to his right. But you can also see the ball going in the goal just inside the left pipe (goalie's left), about halfway up the pipe.

Let's just look at the basic math. The goal is 6' by 6', for a total of 36 square feet. The average-sized goalie, including all his equipment, covers about 9 square feet. If you guess where to put those 9 square feet, then you have about a 25% chance of making the save. This mean that at best, a guessing goalie will stop an average of 1 in 4 shots – not a good save percentage.

Also, note that if opponents see any game film or a scouting report, they can easily tell if a goalie is in the habit of guessing. By the way, most goalies who guess make the same move every time, e.g., they guess low and bring themselves and their stick down, or they guess high and jump. The shooter will give a quick fake, watch the goalie guess, and then dump it past him.

On the other hand, if I have even a tenth of a second to see the shot and make some kind of move to it, then I think I have a better than 1 in 4 chance. Plus no scout will ever see me always guessing low or high. Yes, I have pretty good reflexes, but as a goalie, you presumably do too. Working on your mechanics, watching the ball, not panicking, and intense conditioning will improve your reflexes and help you with 1-on-1's.

Not guessing, but knowing Tendencies: As I mentioned, I never guess where a shot will go, BUT every now and then, I'll find that a certain player has definite tendencies to

190

shoot in certain a place. In that case, I won't guess but will at least know that when he winds up, it's most likely that the shot will go high right or whatever.

For example, for a couple years in summer league, I played against an All American who had a rocket of a shot – 95+ mph - but almost always shot right at my 5-hole, about 2 inches above the ground. When he got the ball out front and wound up, I "cheated" by bending my knees a little more and dropping my stick a bit more than usual. This guy put up some big numbers, but seldom got one past me, and he never caught on that I was anticipating his shot. He's in the Lacrosse Hall of Fame now, and I'm not – but at least I got the better of him for a while. See *Section 17.0* below for more on "getting to know your opponent."

15.0 Dealing With Screens

Screens can make a goalie's life tough. Most opponents will use a screen at least a couple times a game, and some have screens built in as a major part of their offense. Plus there are always accidental screens that happen as players are running around in front of the goal.

Rather than just stand there and not be able to see the ball, there are a few things a goalie can do to be more successful in dealing with screens.

Tendencies: I'll go out on a limb and say that most guys will shoot low when they have a good screen. Why? Well, there's a lot of surface area to get past the midsections of his own teammate (who's setting the screen) and the D-man – so shooting at hip-height isn't usually a good option. And high shots have to get past helmets and at least a couple of sticks that are waving around unpredictably. So the shooter sees a lot more empty space down low, where there are just four skinny legs to deal with (skinnier than the midsection anyway). And on double screens, which a lot of teams use, there's even more mass up high.

Of course, this doesn't mean that the shot will always be low, but it's a tendency to be aware of.

Talk: When I'm screened, I don't yell out "I'm screened! Move that guy over!" If I did that, I'd be letting the ballhandler know that I can't see jack, and now is a great time to shoot. Instead, before the season (and before each game), I tell the defense that when I yell a code word ("Red" or whatever), that means that I'm screened and they need to move their guy over to one side or the other. I don't care which way they move him, just so he's out of my line of vision.

Stance, Position, and What to watch for: If that doesn't work – and it often doesn't against a team that's good at screening – then I:

1) Stay pretty much in my normal stance.

2) Stay on the usual position on the arc (e.g., for when the ball is Right Top, I stand on the arc where I normally would for ball at Right Top.

3) Watch the place where the shooter's stick is most likely to appear as he's shooting.

Let's look at these three items in more detail:

1) Stance: When screened, there's an almost universal tendency among goalies to get out of their normal "ready to save" stance so they can try to peek around the

screen and see the ball. Guys stand straight up, get up on their toes, crouch way down, and/or lean awkwardly way over to the left or right. In these stances, the goalie isn't balanced and can't take a first step as fast as he needs to. As soon as a decent shooter sees a goalie who's unbalanced and not ready to step at a shot, he unloads.

2) Position: Goalies also tend to move too far to their left or right so they can see the shooter better. Again, a good shooter will see that the goalie is out of position and aim for the open net. The goalie is too far over to reach the far corner, even with a fairly good move.

3) What to Watch: I've talked about how important it is to watch the ball, and that's one reason screens can be so effective: The goalie can't stop what he never sees. First, when screened, I try to stay calm and not panic that I can't see the ball. When goalies panic, they forget their solid fundamentals, and don't make good save moves.

Next, I figure out where the ball is going to first appear when the guy shoots. (Note that this is also true for dealing with attackers who hide the ball well before they fire.)

For example, if the ballhandler is carrying the ball high, behind his helmet, then I watch the stick-side place right next to his helmet, because this is where his stickhead will first show up as he shoots. Unless the screener is really tall, this isn't all bad, because the high area usually isn't as screened as the middle, where bulky bodies are in the way. If the screener is tall and I can't see the shooter's helmet, then I just have to watch whatever I can – his hands, elbows, whatever will tell me the approximate height of the stickhead where the shot will come from.

If the ballhandler is carrying the ball lower – say for a sidearm shot, then I watch between his shoulder and waist. If winding up for an underhand shot, then I watch low.

I do peek around a little, as long as it doesn't take me out of a balanced "ready to save" stance.

In summary, it's much more effective to stay in your good stance as much as possible, stay more or less on your usual position on the arc, and watch for where the shooter's stickhead and the ball will next appear.

16.0   Temptation / Baiting

Some people call this "baiting": In summary, what the goalie does is try to tempt or "bait" the attacker to shoot at a certain spot, because the goalie has a great save move to that area.

For example, there are a couple spots that I know I have a really fast move to. I'm not going to reveal what they are, in case there are any opponents out there – but for the sake of argument, let's say that I'm really great at getting to shots aimed at my offside. I've practiced offside moves a million times and have had a lot of success making that save in practice and in games.

Let's say an attacker has the ball Left Front and seems like he wants to shoot. What I'll do is take up my stance farther to my left, so that he can see a lot of empty net to my right (my offside). Ideally, I will have tempted him to shoot to my offside, where I'm really strong. He fires right where I want him to, and I eat it up. Figure 16-1 below is an example of this.

Figure 16-1 – Temptation
Goalie is tempting the ballhandler to shoot to his (goalie's) stick-side

This technique is hard to master but can work really well. First, you have to have a great save move to somewhere, and that takes all the work and practice I've been talking about. Plus you have to try to keep that move a secret. At higher levels, people will scout you, but they often don't pick up when you're "baiting."

Second, you have to pick the right situation. It's easiest when the shooter is a middie who wants to wind up from out front. But you can also use it when an attacker is coming around the corner. For example, if you're really quick at getting your legs together to block low shots, then as he comes around, have your feet farther apart than normal, which shows him a big gaping 5-hole. Be ready to snap your legs together as he fires.

Temptation is a little hard to practice because you can't tell the shooter, "Hey I'm going to bait you – let's see if you fall for it." So you have to kind of work it into practice every now and then and see how you make out.

17.0 Get to Know Your Opponent

If you're playing in high school or college, you'll probably get scouting reports and maybe even game film. If possible, go watch your next opponent play. Use every bit of information you can get to find out as much as you can. After a game, I've asked guys on the other team things like, "So when you played Team X, who was their best shooter? What do I have to watch out for?" and so on. They'll usually give me a lot of great intel.

You want to learn things like:
1) Who are their best shooters? Do they shoot best right- or left-handed, or both?

2) For each shooter, does he shoot bounce shots, high, low, offside, what?

3) Who are their best feeders? Where do they feed from?

4) What offensive set do they use? 2-2-2? 3-2-1?

5) What plays do they like to run: Feed from behind? Clear out for the one on one? Sweeps? Backdoor? Turn the corner and shoot? Screens?

6) What defenses worked against them?

7) What ride do they use?

Once you've learned all this, talk with your coach and defense (including D-middies) about it and plan how to defend ahead of time. For example, if the opponent has one great player who carries the ball a lot and gets most of their goals, you might want to put your best D-man on him, and play him really tight the whole game - you "lock him off," even when he doesn't have the ball.

As goalie, you want to know the tendencies of all their best shooters, so for example, when #8 gets the ball out front, he likes to sweep right, and as soon as he gets free just a little, he plants and wings a sidearm shot offside high. As goalie, you tell your middies to get ready to slide fast onto this guy when he starts to get a step. Plus you can anticipate the high hard one.

Your team needs to plan a specific defense for every offensive set they use. The goalie needs to recognize what offense they're in and call out the defense to use. The same goes for rides. On dead ball clears, if they like to put a man on the goalie, then you might want to have a middie take it.

Your coach will hopefully practice all this during the week before the game, but the goalie needs to take an active part in knowing everything that's going on. The goalie runs the defense on the field, which is 70% of the team, and the coach won't be out there to adjust everything on the fly.

Thorough preparation can save you at least a couple of goals a game, so I try to not get lazy. If you're anything like me, you don't like to get scored on, and planning ahead can be just as important as stepping to the ball.

If you play club ball or youth league, you might not get any scouting reports, and almost certainly no game film. But you, a teammate, coach or parent might be able to get to an opponent's game and take a few notes. If that doesn't happen and I have to go in completely cold, knowing nothing at all about the opposition, I take a few minutes to watch them warming up before the game. I can usually tell who their best players are and share that with my D-men before the first face-off.

At the very least, by the end of the first quarter, you'll know a lot. I always make adjustments as I go along and learn more. And I'll have my D-men make some changes as well – switching who's guarding which attackman, using a different clear, and so on.

Before a game I'll also watch the other goalie warm up. As a goalie, I often see weaknesses that non-goalies don't pick up on. I'll tell my shooters things like, "This guy looks weak on bounce shots to the offside." It's great when one of our shooters comes over to me after a game and says, "Hey, thanks for the tip about his offside. I nailed him twice on that."

18.0   Practice for Goalies

This section is mainly for coaches, since they run the practice, but goalies will learn a few things too.

I hate to say this, but many coaches know next to nothing about how to coach goalies. Many college programs have well-qualified goalie coaches, but most high schools and youth leagues are understandably unable to field a full- or even part-time coach who has played a lot of goalie and really knows how to help a kid get better in the cage. Even coaches who played defense usually have no clue what goes on inside the crease.

So this section will list a few drills that I think will help the average coach to improve his goalies' play.

18.1 Warm-up

I've seen a coach do more damage warming up his goalie in 15 minutes than the opposing team does in a whole game. Most coaches shoot too fast, too soon in the warm-up, from too close in. But without going into all those sins, here's the type of warm-up that works best for me and, I think, for most goalies.

Before warming up, I do some stretching – arms, legs, back, etc. I'll be running a lot in the game, so have to stretch to avoid pulling a hamstring or whatever. Plus, when I make a save move, I go so hard to the ball that it puts a lot of strain on muscles, ligaments and tendons so a little stretching helps.

I also like to take a jog or even just a walk around the field a time or two. This also helps to loosen me up and get the blood flowing without being too strenuous.

Then, wearing all my gear, I throw some passes, first short (10 yards) and easy, and gradually harder and farther, up to about 50 yards. This helps me get my eyes warmed up, meaning that I'm focusing on the ball, but without the stress of a hard shot. It also loosens my arms up and gets me used to catching the ball – and controlling a save is really just an advanced form of catching.

Next I get in the goal for the warm-up. Every goalie may prefer a different sequence, but Stages 1, 2 and 3 are what works for me.

> *Note to coaches: During each of the 3 stages listed below, the coach can give the goalie feedback that focuses on fundamentals and technique: As a coach, make sure the keeper is watching the ball, in a good stance, focusing on the drill, stepping to the ball, and all the other things I've covered in this book. For example, if the goalie is holding his arms too close to his body, stop shooting, get him to put his arms into the right*

position, and then start up again. These bad habits will usually show up in Stage 1, when shots aren't coming at full speed, so get them fixed then, before you move on to shooting harder in Stages 2 and 3.

Feedback is most useful if it's not screamed in anger and frustration. The kid is trying to do his best, but just needs some guidance. Deliver it like a friend, not a maniac.

Stage 1: Easy – the main goals of this stage are to make sure the goalie is:
- Getting into the right stance
- Stepping to the ball
- Watching the ball
- Using good form in his save moves
- Getting his confidence up

The shooter doesn't throw very hard at first.
1) Start at stick-side high, then work "around the clock":
2) Stick-side hip
3) Stick-side low (not a bounce shot)
4) Center low (5-hole)
5) Offside low
6) Offside hip
7) Offside high
8) Straight at the face
9) Straight at the midsection

See Figure 18-1 below:

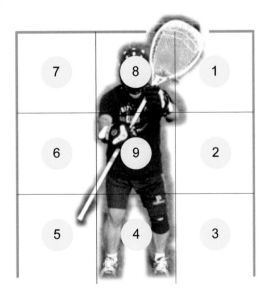

Figure 18-1: Warm-up sequence #1

199

Some goalies prefer a somewhat different sequence:
1) Start stick-side high, then
2) Straight at the face,
3) Offside high,
4) Stick-side hip
5) Straight at the midsection
6) Offside hip
7) Stick-side low (not a bounce shot)
8) Center low
9) Offside low

See Figure 18-2 below:

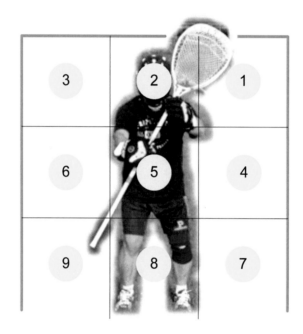

Figure 18-2: Warm-up sequence #2

Regardless of which sequence you use, for this first "easy" stage, the shooter stands out front, about 15 yards away. He shoots while standing still, not running. He can move right and left a few yards, so the goalie will start to move along the arc. The shooter needs to shoot both right- and left-handed if possible. He should also shoot like a real attackman. By this I mean his shot shouldn't be something odd. For example, I've seen a coach who held his stick really high before he shot. Most attackers don't shoot like this in a game, so the goalie is seeing a release point and a type of shot that won't help him much.

Stage 2: Harder - the main goals of this stage are the same as Stage 1: to make sure the goalie is:
- Getting into the right stance,
- Stepping to the ball,
- Watching the ball
- Using good form in his save moves
- Getting his confidence up

But in Stage 2 we're also getting the goalie to speed up.
Plus we'll start in on bounce shots.

The shooter goes through the same sequence as above but shoots harder, though not "all out." After the sequence, he starts shooting bounce shots, first stick side, then 5-hole, then offside. Bouncers need to be high, medium and low in height. During Stage 2, the shooter is still shooting from a standing position, not running or sweeping.

Stage 3: When the coach feels that the goalie is moving well, seeing the ball well, and feeling confident, then it's on to Stage 3. The main goals of this stage are the same as Stages 1 and 2 - to make sure the goalie is:
- Getting into the right stance,
- Stepping to the ball,
- Watching the ball
- Using good form in his save moves
- Getting more confident

Plus in Stage 3 we're also getting the goalie to speed up to the max, to game speed. Also, the shooter will start to run straight in and shoot, sweep and shoot, fake and shoot, everything.

In my experience, these three stages – done in this sequence, every day - will help a goalie get better, without making him gun-shy.

In *Section 19.0 – Pre-Game Prep*, I'll go over some additional stages and drills that can be used before games and/or in practice.

18.2 Muscle memory

I talked about muscle memory in the introduction to this book, but it's so important for practicing that I'll repeat it here:

> **One important note about practicing and drills:** Especially early in your career, one of your main goals is to build the correct "muscle memory" for each key move. For example, when you move to make an offside low save, you want all your muscles – the ones that control your feet, legs, hands, arms, neck, etc. – to be doing the right thing, in the right sequence, at the right time. Having the best muscle memory just

means that you've practiced the correct save move so much that your muscles have "memorized" everything correctly, and you can do the whole thing automatically and really fast.

A basketball foul shot is an example: The best foul shooters do the same thing, move their same muscles the same way (or very close to it) every time. Their muscles have "memorized" what to do.

Likewise, as a goalie, you want to train your muscles to automatically do the right things to make the save. On a shot, seeing the ball leave the stick is the "cue" that should set your muscles into the right moves that they've "memorized." That's one reason you'll see me emphasize watching the ball so much. The faster you can pick up the shot leaving the stick, the faster your muscles can be "cued" to go into the right "memorized" moves.

For me, the best way to build and improve muscle memory is the following:

1) First you have to learn what the correct moves are for each type of shot...There's no point in becoming fast at a bad move, so learn to do it right the first time.

2) Second, with all your gear on but without getting shot at, start to make this move slowly, one step at a time. Go slowly until you think you're doing the move correctly. You probably need somebody – preferably an experienced goalie - to watch and help you make adjustments.

3) Third, without being shot at, repeat the move many times, gradually going faster and faster.

4) Next, get in the cage, and have somebody shoot at you so that you can practice that same move. They can start shooting fairly slowly and gradually increase the speed. Get feedback from an experienced goalie if at all possible.

5) Finally, you get to do all your save moves in practice, scrimmages and games.

I use a similar approach for learning to pass, catch, scoop, dodge and so on:

1) Learn how to do it right.

2) Do it slowly, a step at a time, by yourself, but with a more experienced person watching to give you feedback on your form.

3) Do it faster and faster, and/or harder and harder, until you reach game-level intensity.

4) Do it in game-simulation conditions (drills, practice).

5) Do it in scrimmages, practice and games.

As you read through this book, try this same approach when you come to something new. If you start to build the proper muscle memory early in your career, it'll provide a great foundation for continuing to improve.

When you're warming up during the 3 Stages described above, one thing you're doing – in addition to having fun - is working to improve your muscle memory for making the right save moves on the main types of shots:

1) Straight-on high
2) Straight-on middle
3) Straight-on low
4) Stick-side high,
5) Stick-side hip
6) Stick-side low
7) Offside high
8) Offside hip
9) Offside low

The more you can practice these moves, the better you'll get. But as you practice, and as you warm up, make sure you're getting good feedback from a coach or teammate who can point out when your technique is "off." It takes a lot of time, practice, and dedication to become really good at all these moves. In my experience, the extra work pays off – eventually, you can make an offside low save without even thinking about it.

18.3 Other

The goalie is obviously involved in practice beyond just warming up. I suggest that he does scooping, passing, dodging and similar drills along with the rest of the team. Plus he'll obviously be involved in learning the D packages, Clears, and Man-down D. On most teams, the goalie runs these plays so needs some practice in taking over the drill and, say, running the clear, without a coach telling everybody what to do every 2 seconds.

Some coaches use or recommend special drills just for goalies, such as:

1) Getting in the goal with no stick and getting shot at with tennis balls. This teaches the goalie to step to the ball and move his whole body as he makes the save.

2) During warm-up, using a short stick instead of the goalie stick. This is to help the goalie focus on the ball and on getting the stickhead in position to make the save.

3) Putting sand in the shaft to make it heavier. Same principle as weights on a baseball bat.

4) Having a goalie in full gear, standing facing a wall. Coach behind the goalie throws at the wall and goalie makes the save the rebound off the wall. Helps goalie to pick up the ball from anywhere.

I've heard people say good things about these drills but have never actually used them myself, so can't speak from personal experience. I think that any drill that involves stepping to the ball, watching the ball, and making saves is good. Anything that repeats the fundamentals over and over is invaluable to newer goalies (in their first 2 or 3 years), and also required for those of us who have been around a while.

Time is limited for most of us, so the objective is to pick what works best for you, the goalie. In general, if I had to rank how I've best spent my time, I prefer solid warm-ups (as described above) and lots of game-like play. I also learned a lot from wall ball, especially since I could do it any time, in and out of season, and whether or not anybody else with a stick was around. If I had to choose between a real warm-up and some drill with tennis balls, I'd take the warm-up every time.

Once a goalie has some grasp of and skill in the fundamentals, then there's no substitute for games or game-like drills. Only by playing a lot will he learn all the different things that can happen, make mistakes and learn from them, see and make save moves on all types of shots, get better at "seeing the whole field," throw all the different types of passes from anywhere on the field, learn to keep his cool during fast breaks, and so on. Drills are great for preparing him for some of this, but not for everything that can happen.

18.4 *"Don'ts"*

I've seen a lot of useless drills and approaches that I think do more harm than good to a goalie. Here are a few of the most common:

1) Kamikaze Drill: First and worst, is the "let guys run in on a goalie unguarded and shoot as hard as they can" drill. This is especially bad for new goalies. If you let guys run in and fire away on the goalie, you can easily do two things:

   a) Destroy his confidence: Unguarded shooters winding up from 10 or 15 feet should score most of the time, so if the goalie does this drill too much, he starts to think that he's no good and can't stop anything.

   b) Make him gun-shy: In this drill, the goalie usually gets hit hard a lot. You have to understand that standing in the goal takes some guts in the first place because on every shot, there's the possibility that you'll get hit with the ball. It hurts – there's no way around that. Some guys have a higher tolerance to pain, and some are in such good shape that only the hardest shots hurt much. But for the average teenager who's even in decent shape, getting hit with a hard shot is painful. If it happens too often, his body eventually says "Get out of the way of that thing," instead of "Step to the ball and make the save."

Take this drill off your list. I've been through it a hundred times, and only ended up bruised and annoyed.

Having said that, I think goalies need some sort of game-like one-on-one practice. I suggest starting slow and telling him: For example, "OK, I'm going to come around the corner with my stick high. You come out and nail me." Or "I'm going to come around the corner, with my stick low, and I'll shoot low." Or "I'm coming straight in from Right Top, and I'm going to fake high and shoot low."

The objective here is to build up some confidence and make sure he sticks to solid fundamentals when faced with a one-on-one. Telling him what you're going to do beforehand will help with this. Then you can gradually build up to half- and then full-speed. Finally, you do the drill without telling him what you're going to do. This approach works much better than the "whole team running in and shooting" drill.

2) <u>Unrealistic Warm-ups:</u> I've had coaches who want to do one-on-one warm-ups, close in or on the crease, but they don't wear a helmet, gloves, etc. If you want to have the goalie practice coming out on a guy who's turning the corner from behind, then put on some gear so the keeper can whack you and knock you over. If you're just in shorts and a tee-shirt, he has to hesitate and worry about hurting you, which will teach him nothing. If you don't want to get hit, then find another coach or a player to suit up and do the drill right.

3) <u>Yelling at the goalie:</u> Screaming at your goalie during a practice or game seldom helps. For the goalie, it's bad enough to let a goal in, but even worse to be publicly humiliated by some coach who never made a save in his life. Yes, goalies will make bad passes, will run the clear wrong, and will miss shots they should have stopped. If you've warmed your goalie up properly, at the beginning of the game, he should be in the best physical and mental state possible for him at that time.

As a practice or game unfolds, you have to carefully watch for any deterioration in the goalie's concentration, confidence and fundamentals. When you notice something, draw him aside during a break and get him back on track. For making saves, 95% of the time, you just have to remind him to do one of these things:
   - Watch the ball all the time
   - Get in the right stance
   - Step to the ball

If you notice something important in a game and can't call a time-out, then sure, you have to yell some instructions to him. But do it like a pro, not like some foaming-at-the-mouth psychopath. You just make a fool of yourself, and don't help the goalie – or the team - at all.

If he's throwing bad passes, during the break in the action, correct his fundamentals and have him throw a few. If he's forgotten the clear set-up, figure out what's missing and remind him. If he's not talking loud enough, tell him to speak up so his defense can hear him.

None of this requires any yelling and histrionics. And by the way, at the high school level, probably 60%-70% of goals scored are due to a D-man or a middie screwing up, not because of the goalie. So focus your attention on them too, not just the keeper.

4) <u>Pampering the Goalie:</u> On one end of the spectrum is the coach who tortures and browbeats his goalie all day long, and on the other end is the coddling coach. I've seen this a few times: The coach is so worried that his goalie (who must be a little "off" in the first place) will have a meltdown that he treats him with kid gloves all the time. "Oh no, Jim, you don't have to do that drill. Just stand over there for a while." Or he'll never shoot hard at a goalie because he's worried he might hurt his feelings by scoring. It's true that some goalies – like some middies, attackmen and D-men – aren't all that hard-nosed or are prima donnas who will go into a snit if treated with some discipline.

But in general, I've always wanted to be treated just like any member of the team: I like to do the same drills they do and not be segregated from anything. Yes, I have to warm-up while they're doing something else, but other than that I always ran the same miles, wind sprints and stadium steps; scooped the same ground balls; and threw the same passes.

Occasionally, you'll get a very talented goalie with an "odd" personality. This is ok, and as long as he's doing the drills, practicing hard and not dragging your team down, there's no need to try to "make him straighten up." I've seen a lot of squads rally around a funky guy who brings some fun to the field, rather than the dead serious guy who is all work and no play. The cage attracts some interesting types, and a little offbeat humor never hurt a team.

19.0 Pre-game Prep

Before a game, I think it's good to go through the same routine that the goalie uses before practice. As I mentioned in *Section 18.0*, I start with stretching, then passing, then warm-up.

In practices, after Stage 3 (as described in *Section 18.1*), the coach will have a list of drills to go through, which the goalie will be involved in. But before a game, I recommend Stages 1, 2 and 3, and then add two more stages to get the goalie ready for that first shot fired in anger.

Stage 4: When the goalie is handling Stage 3 well, or at least as well as he ever has, then it's time for Stage 4. The main goals here are:
Put the goalie in some game situations so he's ready for anything.

The shooter will need a couple more guys for this.

- Three guys pass the ball around and then shoot. The goalie will be moving on the arc, making sure he's in the right position, focusing on watching the ball, and of course, making his save moves.

- Passing can be out front, from behind and from GLE. Shooters can receive the feed while standing still or cutting.

- Guy takes the ball behind and comes around the corner for a shot. Goalie has to get in position and make the save.

- Guy comes from X toward the corner but feeds to the back side. Goalie has to get to the backside pipe, get in position and make the save.

In Stage 4, the shooters can shoot fairly hard, but since they have no defenders, I recommend that they hold back on the speed. You don't want to rob the goalie of all the confidence he's been building up during the first 3 stages.

Stage 5: 6 on 6. The main purpose of this stage is to get the goalie completely ready for the game (or this can be incorporated into any daily practice). The offense works the ball around a lot and takes some shots. Since the defense is in, shooters can let fly, but D-men have to be playing hard so the goalie doesn't get shell-shocked. When the goalie makes a save, guys should break downfield for the outlet pass.

After all five stages, the goalie should be ready to go. Depending on how well he's doing, each stage should take about 5 minutes. But if he looks a little lethargic or off his game in Stage 2, for instance, I'd keep working on that stage until he looks readier and more confident.

I like to wrap up Stage 5 about 10 minutes before game-time. This gives the goalie a few minutes to get some water or a sports drink, relax a little, and prepare to "get his head in the game." This is also a chance for the goalie, defense and coach to go over defensive plans one last time, so that it's all fresh in everybody's mind.

Note that I've found 10 minutes to be about right. The goalie doesn't want to sit around for 20 minutes after warm-up because then he'll get cold and fall out of the rhythm he got into during the five Stages. On the other hand, you don't want to end Stage 5 and then immediately line up for the face-off before getting a little break.

Other pre-game prep:
Most of this is obvious, but here are a few other suggestions.

1) Sleep: I try to get a good night's sleep before a game. Sleep-deprived goalies are slower.

2) Fluids: It's best to keep well-hydrated during the whole season, of course, but this is especially true the day before and the day of a game.

3) Food: I just eat normally the day before a game, but make sure I get some good protein and some carbs. I need the fuel from the carbs by the time the 4th quarter rolls around. On game-day, I don't eat anything heavy – mostly fruit, salad, a sandwich. I like being just a little hungry when the game starts. If you eat too close to game-time, a lot of blood and oxygen go to your stomach and digestive tract to deal with the food, and therefore won't be available to your muscles.

4) Heat: If it's hot out, I'll bring a sports drink and eat some potassium-heavy fruit an hour or two before the game, like bananas, oranges or dried apricots. This helps to keep my muscles from cramping.

5) Stimulants: I've seen some goalies downing caffeinated "energy drinks" before games because they think this will speed up their reflexes. I don't know if it's true, but even though I normally drink coffee, I don't have any (or maybe 1 cup) on game-day. I find that it just makes me too wired out and also seems to make me winded more easily when I run a lot.

20.0 Personal Techniques

Throughout this book, I've mentioned a lot of things that I do to practice, get in shape, and play goalie. Most of what I do is fairly orthodox, but over the years I've developed a few techniques that are "out of the box." They work for me, and might not be suited for most players, but I want to include them a) so you can try them if you'd like, and b) to show you that once you've learned the fundamentals thoroughly, you can get creative, try a few experiments, and maybe come up with something new that works well for you.

20.1 My Unorthodox Technique on Low Shots

I taught myself to deal with low and bounce shots in a way that's different from what I described in Sections 7.2 and 7.2.1. You might want to review that material before reading further.

Here's my technique, which I admit is unusual: The first step – out toward the ball – is the same as described above. But what I do differently is then bring my "back" foot right up next to the front foot (see Figures 20-1 and 20-2 below). At the same time, I'm snapping the stickhead down into the shot's path. What this means is that I end up with both feet and legs more or less in the path of the shot, so if my stick gets there a bit late, I have twice as much surface area (both feet and legs instead of one) in the way of the shot. I've even had a lot of shots glance of my front foot, but then be stopped by my back foot as it's coming into place.

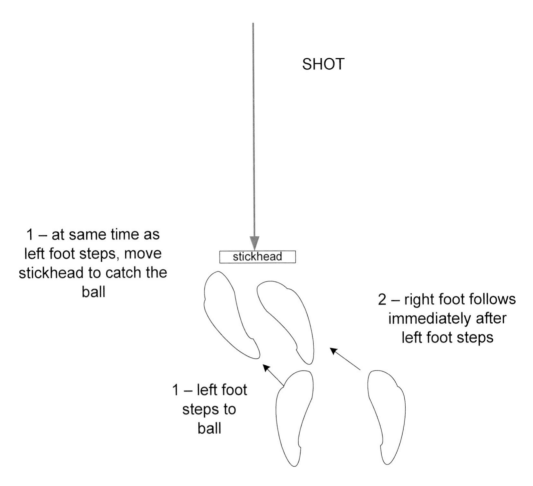

SHOT

stickhead

1 – at same time as left foot steps, move stickhead to catch the ball

2 – right foot follows immediately after left foot steps

1 – left foot steps to ball

Figure 20-1 – My Technique on Low Shots – Not recommended without lots of practice

Figure 20-2 – Feet together on the low save move

To control rebounds, I angle my shins down toward the ground, so that when the ball hits them, it bounces straight down in front of me (most of the time anyway).

I don't recommend this for anybody else, but it might be useful to any goalies who find that, like me, their feet are quicker than their hands. Or you might want to try it for any time you're facing a shooter or two who are bringing some real low heat that you can't catch up to with your stick. There's no shame in making a leg or a foot save – at least it's better than getting beat in the 5-hole all day.

Knowing the move might also improve your ability to stop low shots from guys coming around the corner from behind. As I mentioned above in Section 6.2.4, I try to make the low save with my stick, but use my legs and feet in case I can't get the stick down fast enough.

Another technique is to keep the legs fairly wide apart as the shooter comes in, which might tempt him to go for the 5-hole. You can then use my "low save move" by snapping the legs together, as shown in Figure 20-2 above.

Some goalies are probably shaking with rage or disgust as they read this. "It's heresy!" I agree that it's not for most goalies, but it can be a useful move in some cases, and it works for me.

20.2 Breathing

You may have run across the fact that in martial arts, you exhale sharply when smashing your hand down to break a board. When lifting weights, it's recommended to exhale as you contract the muscle you're working. And who hasn't heard those noisy tennis players grunting as they hit a forehand – that's their way of sharply expelling carbon dioxide just as they swing.

Why is this best? I'm not a scientist, but the general idea is that you inhale, get a lot of oxygen in to the muscles, which then helps them to contract more efficiently. By exhaling as you lift, you expel the carbon dioxide, which doesn't help with the lift, and is a waste product of the work your body is doing. Something like that anyway. My personal experience is that this sharp exhaling seems to increase strength and speed.

One day I was thinking that if I should exhale while lifting, maybe I should try exhaling while making a save move – so I started to practice this. Here's how it works: As a shooter winds up, I take a deep breath, and as I see the shot and start my save move, I exhale sharply. I normally reach the end of my move about the same time as my sharp exhale is over. You might think I'm crazy, but I really believe this makes me faster.

One problem I ran into was that when an attacker has the ball, I'm talking to my defense the whole time, calling out ball location, slides, etc. When the ballhandler gets free of his D-man, I tend to start yelling more, telling somebody to slide and yelling the code word for "He's got a shot! Hit him NOW!" All that yelling involves a lot of exhaling, so I found I was inhaling when the shot finally came, instead of exhaling. My solution has been that if the guy is winding up and none of my longsticks have gotten to him by now, it's too late, he's going to shoot, so I just stop yelling, inhale as he winds, and then exhale fast as I make my move on the shot.

This takes a lot of practice, but makes sense from a scientific, physiological point of view, plus I've had a lot of luck with it. Try it out in warm-up, and if you get the hang of it and it makes you feel faster, try it in scrimmages and games. It takes time to master, but has been worth it to me.

20.3 Re-setting Myself to the Basics

This book has covered a lot of ground, and it may seem overwhelming at times. If you feel like you're sometimes getting lost in the details, here's a good way to clear your mind and re-focus on the few key things that will help you make saves.

I do this before warm-ups, then again before the first face-off, and I repeat the exercise several times during a game – especially before face-offs and as soon as the opponent gets the ball in my end of the field. Here are the four items I concentrate on the most:

1) Focus – pay attention only to what's going on in the game.
2) Watch the ball.
3) Stance – get in a good, solid ready-to-save stance.
4) Step – Step to the ball on every shot.

Failing to do these four things leads to more goals than any other factors that a goalie can control. Doing these four things every time the attackers have the ball will get you a lot of saves.

I have a "code word" that I tell myself that is meant to automatically remind me to do these four things. You can choose whatever word you like. Let's say the word is "Ready." In warm-ups, say "Ready" to yourself: then get in your best stance, focus on the game-play at hand, watch the ball, and then step to each shot. If you do this often enough, you'll eventually get into these good habits every time you say "Ready" to yourself.

I've even heard of some athletes writing their "code word" on their forearm and looking at it whenever they need to "re-set" and get their head back where they want it. This sounds like a pretty good idea, as it provides a visual cue, which can be even more powerful than just saying the word to yourself.

If you prefer some pictures of what I'm talking about, see below:

1) Focus – always be ready, pay attention

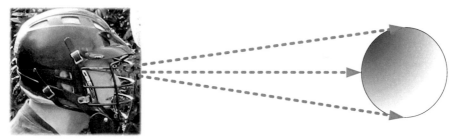

2) Always Watch the BALL

3) Get in a solid Stance

4) Step to the shot

Try this out and see how it works. It's worked well for me, especially after a wild situation, a goal that I should have saved, or any time I find my mind wandering.

21.0 Next Steps

As I mentioned earlier, this book covers a lot of ground. If you're new in the goal, it might seem overwhelming at first. But if you take it in small doses, practice a section at a time, and keep going over the material again and again, then I think you'll start absorbing more and more, and gradually seeing some progress in your game.

Learning to play goalie better is something like building a brick wall. You don't just throw all the bricks up in the air at once and hope they come down in the form of a wall. Likewise, you don't just jump in the cage and suddenly become a great goalie. You start with one "brick" (e.g., "watching the ball"), put it in the right place, makes sure it's level, and then move on to the next (e.g., "the stance"). Every now and then you step back to make sure things are progressing as they should.

And even if you've played goalie for a couple years already, you can still keep getting better at the basics and also work on some of the more advanced techniques.

Whatever your level of experience, as you practice and play more and more, if you're working hard and learning from your mistakes, you'll keep getting better.

Lacrosse is a great sport. I hope you enjoy playing, do your best, make some friends, and show a lot of good sportsmanship. You're joining a long line of goalies – some great, some not so great, but all tough enough to step in the cage. Good luck.

APPENDIX: Back in the Day

One of the things I like about lacrosse is the connection I've always felt with the players and teams of yesteryear. Though not a star, my dad played some lacrosse at St. John's College in the early '30s. He transferred to University of Maryland and, per the rules of the day, was declared ineligible for his remaining years at College Park. However, he apparently hung out with the team and is in the photo below - far left, middle row, in street clothes.

University of Maryland team - 1933

Somewhere in this photo are 5 All Americans from 1933: Norwood Sotharan, Gordon Pugh, Gerald Snyder, Carl Pfau, George Hockensmith

Maybe one of his jobs was to take pictures, as I found the following three photos among his belongings.

Mount Washington vs. Maryland in College Park - 1934

University of Maryland Alumni Game - 1934

Mount Washington vs. Maryland in Baltimore – April 13, 1935

My dad's brother, Tom, was a three-time All-American goalie in the late '40s, also at Maryland. Their cousin (my second cousin), Tommy Gough, was also an All-American in the '40s – but at Hopkins. When the Terps took on the Blue Jays, it was Tom against Tommy, and their mothers (who were sisters) didn't speak to each other for weeks.

My uncle, Tom Hoffecker, Goalie at Maryland, ca. 1948

After graduating from Maryland, "Uncle Warren" (as we called him) went on to play for Mount Washington, the premier lacrosse club in the country for many years. See photo below:

TOM HOFFECKER
Star Mount Washington goalie makes "save" business look easy

The caption reads: 'TOM HOFFECKER – Star Mount Washington goalie makes "save" business look easy' (Baltimore Sun, April 13, 1954).

While Uncle Warren was in the cage for Mt. Washington, I was busy growing up in Chestertown and watching Washington College play a lot of ball. In those years, "the College" had some great All-Americans like Joe Seivold, Mule Jennings, Mickey DiMaggio, Hezzy Howard, and Tommy Allen. They played a beautiful brand of lacrosse, marked by speed, great passing, fluid stickwork and finesse.

In February 1962, I finally got to play myself. Chestertown High School (CHS), on Maryland's Eastern Shore, was a small school and included grades 7 through 12. Even though I was only 12 years old, a 7th grader, I was allowed to try out for the varsity – these were the good old days before rules would have forbidden it. I made first team varsity at center middie – never once thinking about getting between the pipes.

But at the end of the year, we played an exhibition game against "The Old Men" – any local guys past high school age who had played some ball. Our goalie, Ray Gill, wanted to play attack for a change, Coach Tom Elder "volunteered" me to play goalie, and I ended up in the crease for the whole game. Unfortunately, the "Old Men" weren't all that old, and included at least two former All Americans that I know of: Tommy Allen (Honorable Mention as an attackman in 1960) and Don Kelly, a 4-time All-American at attack (1931 through 1934). That sounds like a long time ago, and Coach Kelly was about 50 in 1962 – but in spite of a "trick knee," he still had the smoothest, most deceptive stickwork I've ever faced. For example, he was the first guy I ever saw make the over-the-shoulder-backhanded shot – a rude introduction for a first-time goalie. Tommy liked to shoot and wasn't a bad feeder, either. At Washington College in 1958, he had 15 points in a single game.

The Old Men whipped us, 11-4 or so, but I had a lot of saves. After the game, Tommy Allen tried to get me to go to Boys' Latin – a top program in Maryland then and now. He said he'd get me a scholarship, but I'd already decided to go elsewhere, a place that didn't have a lacrosse team. Skip ahead 5 years, and when I got to Princeton, I still remembered Tommy's encouragement, and figured I might have a shot to play some goalie. In 1968, I started on our freshman team (back when freshman couldn't play varsity) – which was one of the best squads I've ever played on.

The photo below shows some of us Maryland guys from that freshman team. The caption reads: "ALL FROM BALTIMORE – These lacrosse players from the metropolitan area have helped the Princeton Freshmen to victories over Hofstra, Rutgers and Navy." I'm from the Eastern Shore, nowhere near Baltimore, but close enough.

Guys from Maryland (Baltimore Evening Sun, May 8, 1968)

Aside from me, everybody in the photo had great high school careers in the Baltimore area at schools like Gilman, St. Paul's, Boys' Latin, McDonough, City and Severn. In spite of the old wooden sticks, I can assure you that these guys had as much talent as today's players. Unfortunately, for various reasons, many of these talented guys had left the team by 1971, and we were overmatched by powerhouses like Virginia and Maryland. I started that year, but we lost most of our games. After a rough season like that, I was tempted to hang up the spikes and never again get on the wrong end of another fast break. But after college I started playing club ball, and have been at it ever since. Club lacrosse is fun and can get wild – see the three photos below from the Eastern Shore Summer League, 1970's:

Me trying to scare Jay Hadaway (#16).
Jay missed this one, but I'm sure he nailed me the next time.

***Me (#3) trying out the new
"sideways save"***   ***Getting my helmet knocked off***

In the late '80s and early '90s, I played for the Kansas City Lacrosse Club. Below is about the only surviving photo, taken during a tournament that was played at a very empty University of Kansas football stadium. We had a few good players from the East Coast (Salisbury State, Washington College) and won most of our games for several years.

Kansas City Lacrosse Club: ca. 1989

Still in the Cage: Club Lacrosse - 2007

Meanwhile, my son, Tom, started playing goalie and eventually started on the St. Andrew's School (Delaware) varsity. Tom in action:

Tom Hoffecker – 2005

And so the long chain continues – from my dad at St. John's in the early '30s, to my Uncle Warren at Maryland in the '40s, to me ('62 to '08), and finally to Tom. Not a bad 75 years of lacrosse.

Made in the USA
San Bernardino, CA
29 April 2015

About the Author

John Kimble has 25 years of basketball coaching experience. Most recently, he served as the head basketball coach at Crestview (FL) High School for 10 years. During Kimble's tenure, the team averaged almost 18 wins each season (excluding his first year at the helm).

Kimble began his basketball coaching career as an assistant basketball coach at Lexington (IL) High School, serving as the head freshman coach, the head freshman-sophomore coach, and the assistant varsity coach. During his one season at Lexington, the three squads each lost only two games, while amassing an overall 61-6 record. The varsity won the conference, regional, sectional, and super-sectional state tournament championships before losing in the state tournament's Elite Eight.

The following year, Kimble took the head basketball coaching position at Deland-Weldon (IL) High School, where the varsity accumulated a five-year record of 91-43 that included two regional championships, two regional runner-ups, and one sectional tournament runner-up. Next, he moved to Dunlap (IL) High School for five years. His overall 90-45 record at Dunlap included two regional runners-up, one regional, one sectional, and one super-sectional championship and a final second-place finish in the Illinois Class A State Tournament.

Kimble then moved to Florida, where he became an assistant basketball coach at Central Florida Community College in Ocala, Florida. The next year, he became the offensive coordinator in charge of the overall offense. For the next two years, he retained that offensive coordinator responsibility while also becoming an associate head coach, with a two-year record of 44-22. CFCC's overall record during Kimble's four years there was 73-58.

Kimble has worked 90 weeks of basketball camps and has spoken at several coaching clinics and camps. He also has had articles appear in publications such as *The Basketball Bulletin of the National Association of Basketball Coaches, The Scholastic Journal, Winning Hoops,* and *Basketball Sense,* and has contributed articles and diagrams to two different editions of the book *Coaching Basketball.*

Kimble is currently teaching several business classes at Crestview (FL) High School, still studying the game, and still writing basketball articles and books.

You begin the drill by not allowing any player to shoot or dribble. You advance it to allowing 03, 04, 05, or 06 to shoot or dribble. You progress further by then allowing any of the six to shoot, dribble, or pass (except no up pass from the corner to the wing on the same side of the court). If your defenders have mastered their slides and can effectively carry them out in the last two drills without allowing a shot to be taken, your defense will be of championship caliber.

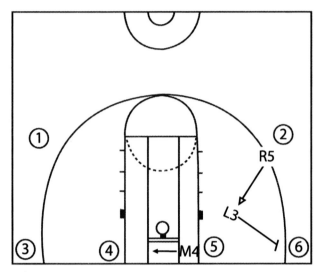

Diagram 12.22